# Cromwell

## PETER YOUNG

*None climbs so high as he
who knows not whither he is going*

# Oliver
# Cromwell

## by Peter Young

INTERNATIONAL
PROFILES

Oliver Cromwell
© Brigadier Peter Young, D.S.O., M.C., M.A., F.S.A., F.R.Hist.S., F.R.G.S., 1968

INTERNATIONAL PROFILES

*General Editor:* EDWARD STORER

*English language editions published in:*
GREAT BRITAIN, EUROPE AND SOUTH AMERICA
by Morgan-Grampian Books Limited
28 Essex Street, Strand, London, W.C.2

*Series Design:* Melvyn Gill     *Pictorial Research:* F. G. Thomas
*Colour Plates:* Photoprint Plates Limited, Wickford, Essex, and W. S. Cowell Limited, Ipswich, Suffolk
*Covers:* George Over Limited, London and Rugby
*Paper:* Frank Grunfeld (Sales) Limited, London
*Text and Binding:* Butler and Tanner Limited, London and Frome

# Preface

1. *Oliver Cromwell, from the Lord Protector Medal by Thomas Simon, 1653* (National Portrait Gallery)

Like Warwick's my sympathies are Royalist. Perhaps this is a re-action against the Parliamentarian leanings of successive genera-tions of historians, including S. R. Gardiner, Sir Charles Firth and Godfrey Davies. Perhaps it is that one who has held the King's commission is apt to look askance at those who raised a rebellion against their sovereign. Whatever its cause I am aware of my bias, and, having declared it, do not mean to let it have full rein. Rather I will try to observe Cromwell's briefing to Mr Lely and paint his picture truly like him: 'warts and everything'.

1

2. *Robert Cromwell, Oliver Cromwell's father* (Mansell Collection)

> I was by birth a gentleman, living neither in any considerable
> height nor yet in obscurity.

OLIVER CROMWELL

*Part 1*

# The Man

3. *Cromwell House, High Street, Huntingdon. The house was granted to the Cromwell family at the Dissolution and is said to be the birthplace of Oliver Cromwell* (Radio Times Hulton Picture Library)

Oliver Cromwell represented the younger branch of a family whose fortunes had been made by Thomas Cromwell, Earl of Essex, the despoiler of the monasteries. Loyalty to his patron had induced Oliver's great-grandfather, Richard Williams, to change his name. Oliver's father, who was M.P. for Huntingdon (1593) and a Justice of the Peace, had an estate worth about £300 a year and was, therefore, fairly well off.

The seeds of Cromwell's Puritanism were sown early. He had his education at the Free School of Huntingdon and at Sidney Sussex College, Cambridge.* At the first his master was the Reverend Thomas Beard, whose beliefs were set forth in *The Theatre of God's Judgments*. From him, no doubt, Cromwell imbibed his notions

* He matriculated on 23 April 1616 and went down on the death of his father in June 1617. He *may* have studied thereafter at Lincoln's Inn.

that the Pope was Antichrist and that crime is inevitably followed by punishment. At the second he was in 'a hotbed of Puritanism', though he did not remain long.

Though narrowly religious, Cromwell's education was not altogether inadequate. Nor did he underrate its value. It was his opinion that cosmography, mathematics and a little history 'fit for public services for which a man is born'. He had enough Latin to converse in that tongue with the Dutch Ambassador, and greatly valued not only King James's Bible but Raleigh's *History of the World*: 'Tis a body of History, and will add much more to your understanding than fragments of story.'

Standing 5 feet 10 inches, Cromwell was above the average height, and was 'well compact and strong'. As a young man he enjoyed 'horse and field exercise, football, cudgels, and other manly sports'.

To study Samuel Cooper's marvellous miniature one would suppose that a robust body was matched by a calm and reflective mind. But in fact under that rugged exterior he seems to have been rather temperamental. Contemporary doctors described him as 'valde melancholicus' and as 'a most splenetic man'. On the other hand he 'loved an innocent jest', and though he had a hot temper it was well under control. Perhaps the best description of him comes from Maidstone, his steward during the Protectorate:

> His head so shaped as you might see it a storehouse and shop both of a vast treasury of natural parts. His temper was exceeding fiery, . . . but the flame of it, kept down for the most part, was soon allayed with those moral endowments he had. He was naturally compassionate towards objects in distress. . . . A larger soul, I think, hath seldom dwelt in a house of clay.

At first Cromwell cared but little for his appearance. In November 1640 Warwick saw him making a speech in Parliament 'very ordinarily apparrelled' in a 'plain cloth suit, which seemed to have been made by an ill country tailor'. He had evidently cut himself shaving for there was 'a speck or two of blood upon his little band which was not much larger than his collar'. Worse still, in the Royalist courtier's eyes, 'his hat was without a hatband'. For the rest, 'his countenance was swollen and reddish, his voice sharp and untunable and his eloquence full of fervour'.

4. *Elizabeth Steuart Cromwell, Oliver Cromwell's mother* (National Portrait Gallery)

As Protector, Cromwell got a better tailor, and the same witness speaks of his 'great and majestic deportment and comely presence'. Nor was plain black his only wear. In 1654 his wardrobe included a musk-coloured suit, and a coat richly embroidered with gold.

Cromwell was born at Huntingdon on 25 April 1599 and for nigh on thirty years lived a life in no way more remarkable than those of contemporaries in his own walk of life. He married Elizabeth Bourchier (22 August 1620) and raised a numerous brood.* In early manhood he gave little evidence of piety, though doubtless Warwick went too far—at least by twentieth-century standards—when he wrote of his spending his time 'in a dissolute course of life in good fellowship and gaming'. In 1629 he was elected to the third Parliament of King Charles I as member for Huntingdon. This was the assembly which drew up the Petition of Right and declared the illegality of arbitrary imprisonment and taxation without the consent of Parliament. Cromwell's maiden speech seems to have been one in which he spoke on behalf of the free preaching of Puritan doctrine. Perhaps he had already suffered the agonies of that spiritual conversion which led him later (1638) to exclaim: 'You know what my manner of life hath been. Oh, I lived in darkness and hated light. I was a chief—the chief of sinners. This is true; I hated Godliness, yet God had mercy on me.'
    The King parried the Parliamentary onslaught of Sir John Eliot and his associates by dissolving Parliament, and ruling for the next eleven years without its aid. During these years Cromwell played some part in public affairs, serving as a J.P., and opposing the King in the dispute over the draining of the fens (1636). But his chief occupation was farming at St Ives, Huntingdonshire, whither he moved in 1631. Nevertheless by 1636 he was sufficiently well known for the Bishop of Lincoln to describe him as a spokesman of sectaries. The same year his uncle, Sir Thomas Steward, died, leaving him most of his estate. Cromwell, who inherited the post of farmer of the tithes of Ely Cathedral, was now really well-to-do. The next few years were certainly the calmest and perhaps the happiest of his life, secure both in

* Robert (1621–39); Oliver (1623–44); Bridget (1624–?); Richard (1626–1712); Henry (1628–1674); Elizabeth (1629–?); Mary (1637–?); Frances (1638–?).

6. TOP LEFT: *Henry, fourth and youngest son of Oliver Cromwell* (Radio Times Hulton Picture Library)    7. TOP RIGHT: *Mary, third daughter of Oliver Cromwell* (Mansell Collection)

8. BOTTOM: *Bridget, eldest daughter of Oliver Cromwell* (Mansell Collection)

9. TOP LEFT: *Richard, third son of Oliver Cromwell* (Radio Times Hulton Picture Library)   10. TOP RIGHT: *Frances, fourth and youngest daughter of Oliver Cromwell* (Mansell Collection)

11. BOTTOM: *Elizabeth, second daughter of Oliver Cromwell* (Mansell Collection)

conscience and estate. It is the period recalled in Marvell's well-known lines:

> From his private gardens, where
> He lived reservèd and austere,
> As if his highest plot
> To plant the bergamot.

It would be fascinating to know whether echoes of Lützen and Breitenfeld penetrated to Oliver's country retreat, stirring the war-like spirit as yet latent within him. We are on surer ground in speculating that his indignation was roused by such Star Chamber cases as that of Prynne, Burton and Bastwick, condemned to suffer the pillory, loss of their ears and solitary confinement (1637). Nor can he have heard with indifference of the fate of 'Freeborn John' Lilburne, who was condemned to be whipped at the cart's tail, pilloried and gagged, despite the fact that he was of gentle birth.

The Ship Money case touched Cromwell more nearly. The defendant, John Hampden, was his cousin, and his condemnation seemed to give the Crown limitless power over the lives and purses of all Englishmen. Even so, to sectaries or independents like Cromwell, the religious policy of Charles's government was yet more objectionable than his constitutional and legal ideas. Archbishop Laud's endeavours to ensure propriety—'the beauty of holiness'—in the services of the Anglican Church were not much better than Popery to a man of Cromwell's persuasion.

The Englishman of the mid-seventeenth century was far from being the phlegmatic John Bull beloved of later caricaturists. He was swift to resent an injury, quick to lug out his sword. It is to his credit that he could summon the patience to stomach both Ship Money and the Laudian Visitation at the same time. The Scots were less tolerant. Rather than accept the book of Common Prayer they signed the National Covenant (February 1638) and resolved to die in defence of their religion.

Cromwell, who had as yet done so little in the world, foresaw that the time was coming when he must 'put forth himself in the cause of his God'. He confided this feeling in a letter to a cousin whom he loved, Mrs St John. His language was mystical, but his meaning plain.

Truly, then, this I find; That He giveth springs in a dry and barren wilderness where no water is, I live . . . in Mesheck, which signifies *Prolonging*; in Kedar, which signifieth *Blackness*: yet the Lord forsaketh me not. Though He do prolong, yet He will (I trust) bring me to His tabernacle, to His resting-place. My soul is with the congregation of the first-born, my body rests in hope, and if here I may honour my God either by doing or by suffering, I shall be most glad.

The time for suffering was not yet, but the First Bishops War (1639) compelled the King to summon Parliament in order to pay for the conquest of Scotland. Cromwell, who sat as member for Cambridge, was doubtless one of those who welcomed Pym's catalogue of grievances with cries of 'a good oration'. No doubt he heartily approved the determination to vote no money until 'the liberties of the house and the Kingdom were cleared'. On this rock the Short Parliament (5 April to 5 May 1640) foundered, for seeing that no money was forthcoming the King dissolved it.

In the North the new Scots Army proved more warlike than the still newer English one. So far from reducing the rebels of his other kingdom Charles now found them across the border, comfortably ensconced in Northumberland and Durham. In order to pay them to go away he was compelled to summon the Parliament that was to bring about his downfall. In this, the Long Parliament, Oliver Cromwell, though not a leader of the first rank, was from the outset a person of some importance. About a quarter of the members had sat in the Parliament of 1628 and he was one of them. And he had allies: no less than eleven close relations, among them Hampden and Oliver St John. An influential group kept a common table at Pym's lodgings in Westminster, and it is likely that Cromwell was one of it, for already, despite his somewhat uncouth appearance, his moral strength was appreciated by the leaders of the popular party. The subtle and perceptive Hampden told Lord Digby, who was not yet of the Court party: 'That slovenly fellow . . . who hath no ornament in his speech . . . if we should ever come to have a breach with the King (which God forbid) in such case will be one of the greatest men of England.'

Cromwell was not one of the Five Members whose attempted

arrest hastened the final breach between Whitehall and Westminster.* Nevertheless Oliver was from the first an active supporter of 'King Pym'. It fell to him, for example, to move the second reading of the Triennial Act (30 December 1640), by which the King was bound to call a Parliament every third year. His interest in religious affairs was exemplified by a violent attack on the Bishops (9 February 1641).

His uncertain temper was again in evidence during another dispute over the draining of the fens (May 1641). Crossed in committee he answered Lord Mandeville with 'much indecency and rudeness'. Less than two years were to pass before Cromwell was to find himself serving under this same nobleman, who, as Earl of Manchester, was to command the Army of the Eastern Association.

In September there was an important debate on the 'ordinance against Innovations in the Worship of God', a debate whose importance was that it emphasized the breach between Anglican and Nonconformist. At this time Cromwell's attitude was summed up in the words 'I can tell you, sirs, what I would not have; though I cannot, what I would'. And what he would not have was the Book of Common Prayer.

The division between Anglican and Independent in the House, and the withdrawal of the Scots Army, bade fair to bring a reaction in favour of the King. It was a fleeting moment, swiftly dispelled by horrible news from Ireland where bloody rebellion had broken out. There were those who reported that the insurgents were acting in the King's name. In Parliament the two sides vied with each other to display their determination to suppress the rebels. Cromwell's subscription was £500. It seems unlikely that he knew much about the country which one day was to feel his heavy hand. Hatred of Popery was doubtless the motive for this generous contribution.

The great debate on the Grand Remonstrance was the next milestone on the road to Civil War. This was a sort of catalogue of wrongs, real and imagined, going back to the accession of King Charles in 1625.

*They were John Hampden, Sir Arthur Hesilrige, Denzil Holles, John Pym and William Strode. In addition one member of the Upper House was proscribed, Lord Mandeville, soon to be Earl of Manchester.

Cromwell, whose part was no more dramatic than the explanation of the old fen drainage grievance, thought there would be but little opposition. He underestimated the strength of Royalist or Anglican feeling against the ecclesiastical clauses in the Remonstrance. In fact members nearly came to blows during the night of 22 November, and Sir Philip Warwick thought, 'We had all sat in the valley of the shadow of death; for we, like Joab's and Abner's young men, had catcht at each others' locks, and sheathed our swords in each others' bowels, had not the sagacity and great calmness of Mr Hampden by a short speech prevented it . . .'

Some 245 members were absent, and Pym, who had seen to it that all his party were present, was able to carry the Remonstrance by eleven votes (159–148).* Though, thanks to Hampden, he had succeeded in doing so without bloodshed, he had nevertheless brought war closer, for the Royalist and Anglican members were not prepared to accept his ecclesiastical policy without resistance.

During the next half-year England drifted towards war, and as violence loomed nearer, Cromwell, who was nothing if not practical, began to show an interest in things military. That the King was prepared to use force had been clearly demonstrated on 4 January 1642, when at the head of 400 officers and pensioners, armed with pistol and partisan, Charles had attempted to seize and impeach the Five Members. This breach of privilege, which Parliament was soon to declare seditious, made war virtually inevitable, for now Pym and his friends 'fell to raising of monies under pretence of the relief of Ireland' (Clarendon).

Foiled at Westminster the King departed to York where he forbade by proclamation any muster of the trained bands or militia without his consent (27 May). Parliament, which now consisted of some three hundred members of the Commons with thirty of the Lords, countered with the Nineteen Propositions, claiming control of military, naval, foreign, and ecclesiastical affairs besides the right to appoint ministers, councillors and judges. Pym must surely have appreciated that such an ultimatum could lead to war. If he accepted the risk he must have calculated that his adherents were readier for the ordeal than those that followed Charles Stuart.

* The original members of the Long Parliament numbered 552.

> And thou the War and Fortune's son
> March indefatigably on . . .
>
> ANDREW MARVELL

*Part 2*

# The Soldier

14. *The Palace of Whitehall,* circa *1650, from a print by Israel Silvestre* (Radio Times Hulton Picture Library)

Cromwell entered upon his military career as captain of a troop of horse, a rank which he owed, not to any previous experience in the Art of War, but to his standing amongst the followers of John Pym. In the Parliamentarian army of 1642 there were few enough colonels of foot or captains of horse who had smelt powder, and of those amateurs few indeed were to take to soldiering with the fervour of forty-three-year-old Cromwell. His progress proved truly meteoric. Early in 1643 the old captain became a middle-aged colonel, and by the autumn of that year he was a young lieutenant-general.

Those who consider that his remarkable progress is attributable to a shortage of talent among the Parliamentarian high command, should reflect that during his nine years' soldiering Cromwell won a series of victories which no British general was to eclipse until the great Duke of Marlborough came on the scene. The Royalist armies which he defeated, though often short of money and weapons, were by no means to be despised, for they were well-officered and their morale was firmly planted in a conscious loyalty to Crown and Mitre, the old order. Their commanders, men like Goring, Langdale, Cavendish and Sir Arthur Aston, were brave, hard-fighting men, who meant business; Rupert, for one, had a touch of genius, while David Leslie, the Scots commander at Dunbar, was a general of European reputation.

From the outset Cromwell's approach to soldiering was thoroughly practical, as if he understood his weaknesses as well as his assets. Knowing nothing of war or of training cavalry—a complicated business—Cromwell selected men who had probably served on the Continent as his lieutenant and his cornet. Their names were Cuthbert Baildon and Joseph Waterhouse. The quartermaster was Cromwell's brother-in-law, John Desborough. But although he was not against employing a relative, he let his own son, Oliver, serve his first campaign as cornet to Lord St John. The obvious explanation is that he kept the two senior appointments in his troop for professional soldiers.

From the first, Cromwell's success lay in his instinctive skill in what is now called personnel selection. While too many of his fellows in the Earl of Essex's army were content to enlist 'old decayed servingmen and tapsters and such kind of fellows', Cromwell was more ambitious and, as Richard Baxter tells us, took trouble 'to get religious men into his troop'. Cromwell himself described the Cavalier troopers as 'gentlemen's sons, younger sons and persons of quality', who had 'honour and courage and resolution in them'. These he met with men 'of greater understanding than common soldiers and therefore more apprehensive of the importance and consequence of war' to whom 'the public felicity' was more important than money.

In Baxter's view Cromwell strove in this way to avoid 'those disorders, mutinies, plunderings and grievances of the country which deboist [debauched] men in armies are commonly guilty of'.* In the Edgehill campaign of 1642 the Parliamentarian cavalry, with a few notable exceptions, proved both cowardly and inefficient, and though it fell to Cromwell's lot to take but little part in

---

* Baxter names Aires, Desborough, Berry and Evanson as types of this valiant troop.

16

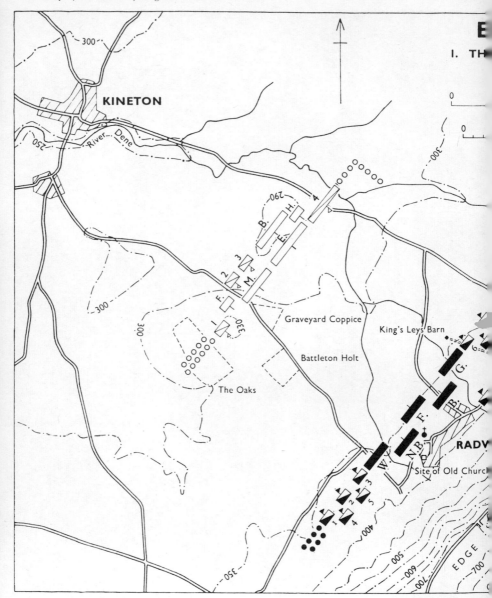

# EHILL

## IES DEPLOYED

ne Mile

1/2    3/4    1

Yards

1000    1500

350

400

USHER

400

500

600
700
600
700
600

HILL

## KEY

### ROYALISTS

HORSE    FOOT    DRAGOONS   ARTILLERY

• • •    ·|· ·|· ·|·

W.—HENRY WENTWORTH.
N.B.—SIR NICHOLAS BYRON.
F. —RICHARD FEILDING.
B. —JOHN BELASYSE.
G. —CHARLES GERARD.
L. —WILLIAM LEGGE'S FIRELOCKS.

1. LORD WILMOT'S REGT.
2. LORD GRANDISON'S REGT.
3. EARL OF CARNARVON'S REGT.
4. LORD DIGBY'S REGT.
5. SIR THOMAS ASTON'S REGT.
6. PRINCE MAURICE'S REGT.

7. PRINCE RUPERT'S REGT.
8. PRINCE OF WALES' REGT.
9. KING'S LIFEGUARD.
10. SIR JOHN BYRON'S REGT.
11. GENTLEMEN PENSIONERS.

### PARLIAMENTARIANS

HORSE    FOOT    DRAGOONS or   ARTILLERY
                 MUSKETEERS

o o o o    ·|· ·|· ·|·

M.— SIR JOHN MELDRUM'S BDE.
E. — CHARLES ESSEX'S BDE.
B. — THOMAS BALLARD'S BDE.

F. — SIR WILLIAM FAIRFAX'S REGT.
H. — DENZIL HOLLES' REGT.

1. LORD FIELDING'S REGT.
2. SIR PHILIP STAPLETON'S REGT.
3. SIR WILLIAM BALFOUR'S REGT.

4. SIR JAMES RAMSEY'S WING.

MODERN COPSES SHOWN:

MODERN CHURCH SHOWN:

the fighting, he saw enough to confirm him in his view that the Parliamentarians needed men 'of a spirit that is likely to go on as far as gentlemen will go'.

The choice of horses was scarcely less important than the selection of personnel. Cromwell and Desborough no doubt had their own horses, and so in all probability did some of his men, since many were freeholders or their sons. Even so it was customary in the Parliamentarian army to give their cavalry commanders mounting money. They were not expected to provide their own horses, arms and saddlery.* A trooper's arms, offensive and defensive, cost about £5,† while the price of a horse varied between £5 and £10. Cromwell's men were 'harquebusiers',‡ a type of cavalry armed and mounted not unlike the heavy cavalry of later days, Napoleon's cuirassiers or our own Household Cavalry. They wore the triple-barred, lobster-tailed helmet, or pot, back and breast-plates, and a buff coat. Their offensive armament included a long stiff straight sword and a pair of pistols. They did not have carbines.

The armies of the Civil Wars included cuirassiers, who wore three-quarter armour, but these were not very numerous.§ Troopers equipped like Cromwell's men were therefore the normal cavalry on each side. They would be expected not only to take their place in the line of battle, but to do the outpost, escort and reconnaissance duties upon which the security of any army must depend.

Cromwell's men were trained to advance to the attack, riding knee to knee at 'a good round trot'. The idea was to keep the men firmly under control so as to enable them to rally quickly after a mêlée. Royalist troops, though they sometimes seem to have fought in the same style, did not do so invariably. At Hopton Heath (19 March 1643), for example, the Cavaliers' first attack is described as 'a very fierce charge, French like'.

Describing his regiment, Cromwell once declared: 'They are no Anabaptists, they are honest sober Christians.' It is not likely that

* The sums allowed to cavalry officers for these purchases were: Captain £140, Lieutenant £60, Cornet £50, Quartermaster £30. (First and Davies, p. 19.)
† *Ibid.*, p. 18.
‡ Despite the fact that the harquebus had gone out of use.
§ Sir Arthur Hesilrige's famous regiment, the 'Lobsters', are an example, but generally cuirassiers were only found in the Lifeguard troops of the various generals.

men of this sort were particularly hard to control, but whether they were or not their commander stood no nonsense. At Huntingdon in April he had two deserters whipped in the market-place and then 'turned off as renegadoes'. In May 1643 a London weekly newspaper recorded of his new regiment that 'no man swears but he pays his twelve pence; if he be drunk he is set in the stocks, or worse, if one calls the other "Roundhead" he is cashiered; insomuch that the countries where they come leap for joy of them, and come in and join with them. How happy were it if all the forces were thus disciplined.'

Promoted colonel when the armies went into winter quarters at the end of the Edgehill campaign, Cromwell had a relatively peaceful period in which to raise his regiment. East Anglia, where he raised his men, was strongly Parliamentarian, but though his officers included Major Edward Whalley, his cousin, Captain Valentine Walton, his nephew, and his son, Oliver, himself now a captain, the gentry did not come forward in sufficient numbers to fill all the commissioned ranks. Cromwell tackled this problem in his usual practical way. His letter to the Suffolk committee (28 September 1643) puts his point of view:

> It had been well that men of honour and birth had entered into these employments, but why do they not appear? Who would have hindered them? But seeing it was necessary the work must go on, better plain men than none, but best to have men patient of wants, faithful and conscientious in the employment, and such, I hope, these will approve themselves to be.

A month earlier (29 August) he had revealed to the same committee his views on training and leadership:

> I beseech you be careful what captains of horse you choose, what men be mounted; a few honest men are better than numbers. Some time they must have for exercise. If you choose godly honest men to be captains of horse, honest men will follow them. . . . I had rather have a plain russet-coated captain *that knows what he fights for, and loves what he knows,** than that which you call a gentleman and is nothing else. I honour a gentleman that is so indeed.

His russet-coated officers included his Captain-Lieutenant, James Berry, who had been a clerk in a Shropshire ironworks, but was

* Author's italics.

one day to be a major-general, Robert Swallow and Ralph Margery.

Cromwell's first serious action seems to have been the fight at Grantham (13 May 1643) in which Lord Willoughby of Parham, Sir John Hotham and he worsted the Cavaliers under Lieutenant-General Charles Cavendish. The only account of the fight, a brief one, comes from Cromwell himself. It was a strange affair. The Roundheads had twelve troops, some of which were 'so poor and broken, that you shall seldom see worse'. The two sides stood drawn up just beyond musket range of each other, and remained stationary for about half an hour, while their dragoons exchanged pot shots. The Roundhead leaders then evidently held a Council of War in the saddle and '. . . they not advancing towards us, we *agreed*\* to charge them, and advancing the [main] body after many shots on both sides, came on with our troops a pretty round trot, they standing firm to receive us, and our men charging fiercely upon them, by God's providence they were immediately routed, and ran all away, and we had the execution of them two or three miles.' This affair cost the Cavaliers 145 men and the Parliamentarians 'but two at the most'. This may have been Cromwell's very first charge. Be that as it may, it was a valuable lesson in minor tactics. Incidentally it shows that the bulk of the casualties were not sustained in the charge or the mêlée, but in the pursuit that followed.

Cromwell's next serious affair was the fight at Gainsborough some ten weeks later. By this time he was handling his unit with the confidence of a veteran.

On this occasion Sir John Meldrum, a Scots veteran, commanded the Parliamentarians some 1,200 strong, and Cromwell with his regiment, now consisting of six or seven troops, brought up the rear. Cavendish's 'Forlorn Hope' was driven back up a steep hill where the Royalist main body was deployed with three regiments in the first line and with Cavendish's own regiment, described as a very strong one, which probably means over 400 men, acting as a reserve.

The Royalist charge caught the Roundheads while they were still endeavouring to put their men in order and so caught them at a

\* Author's italics.

disadvantage. These Parliamentarians by now knew better than to receive a charge at the halt and, as Cromwell himself puts it:

In such order as we were, we charged their great body, I having the right wing. We came up horse to horse, where we disputed it with our swords and pistols a pretty time, all keeping close order, so that one could not break the other. At last, they a little shrinking, our men perceiving it, pressed in upon them, and immediately routed this whole body, some flying on one side, others on the other of the enemy's reserve; and our men, pursuing them, had chase and execution about five or six miles.

With the Royalists' reserve still intact the fight might now have swung their way, had it not been for two of the Parliamentarian commanders, who had the wit to hold back some of their men from the chase. One of these was probably Captain Edward Ayscoghe, for four troops of his Lincoln men rallied to face Cavendish's right flank. The other was Oliver Cromwell, who formed three of his troops in a body facing the Royalists' left wing.

The twenty-three-year-old Cavalier general was now in something of a quandary. He decided to dispose first of the Lincoln men—probably the stronger of his two opponents—and, charging, routed them. Unfortunately it did not occur to him to leave part of his regiment to amuse Cromwell, who describes the inevitable outcome.

I immediately fell on his rear . . . which did so astonish him, that he gave over the chase, and would fain have delivered himself from me, but I pressing on forced them down an hill, having good execution of them, and below the hill, drove the General with some of his soldiers into a quagmire, where my captain-lieutenant [James Berry] slew him with a thrust under his short ribs. The rest of the body was wholly routed, not one man staying upon the place.

The day's work was not done. Pushing on, Meldrum relieved Gainsborough only to find that the Earl of Newcastle, with at least five regiments of foot and a great body of horse, was at hand. The Parliamentarian advanced guard fell back in disorder, and there was nothing for it but to carry out a fighting withdrawal in the face of ever-increasing numbers. Often within carbine shot of the enemy, Cromwell's regiment and the Lincoln men fell back by alternate squadrons, getting away, thanks to their coolness, 'without the loss of two men'. Cromwell generously gave much of the credit to his major, Whalley, and to Ayscoghe. 'Sometimes the one . . . faced the enemy, sometimes the other, to the exceeding Glory of God be it spoken, and the great honour of those two gentlemen, [they] with this handful faced the enemy so and dared them to their teeth in at least eight or nine several removes.' This was a handsome tribute, but in truth the day was Cromwell's own. With less than a year's military service he was handling his squadrons with the coolness of a practised veteran.

The Earl of Manchester was now forming the Army of the Eastern Association, and in this Cromwell was nominated one of the four colonels of horse (10 August 1643). His growing reputation ensured that the post of lieutenant-general of the horse should fall to him. He was well known alike to friend and foe and in his next action, Winceby fight, came near to paying for his hard-won glory with his life.

The Parliamentarians, singing Psalms as they advanced at their usual 'good round trot', were received by two volleys from some dismounted dragoons. A shot killed Cromwell's horse, and as he struggled from under it Sir Ingram Hopton rode at him and struck him down. Before he could second his blow some Roundhead trooper slew the Cavalier.

Oliver lost no time in mounting 'a poor horse in a soldier's hands', but he was too late to play much part in the rest of the action. The second charge, which won the day, was led by Sir Thomas Fairfax, the hard-fighting Yorkshire general, whose reputation at that time stood even higher than Oliver's.

The Eastern Association enjoyed a relatively peaceful winter (1643–44) and since the Earl of Manchester, 'a sweet meek man', allowed Cromwell 'to guide all the army at his pleasure' (Baillie), there was harmony at headquarters. It was not to last, for the lieutenant-general did not get on with the commander of the foot, Sergeant-Major-General Lawrence Crauford, who was an unbending Presbyterian Scot. Cromwell was an Independent and the two seemed to take an unholy pleasure in cashiering officers of the other faction. In a well-known letter Cromwell put his point of view in the case of Crauford's lieutenant-colonel.

Ay, but the man is an Anabaptist. Are you sure of that? Admit he be, shall that render him incapable to serve the public? He is indiscreet. It may be so, in some things, we have all human infirmities. I tell you, if you had none but such indiscreet men about you, and would be pleased to use them kindly, you would find [them] as good a fence to you as any you have yet chosen.

Sir, the State, in choosing men to serve them, takes no notice of their opinions, if they be willing faithfully to serve them, that satisfies.

Here spoke the voice of sweet reason, and it is a pity to have to point out that Cromwell himself got rid of at least half a dozen officers, who were 'not Brownists, or of such like sects'. By so doing he incurred much criticism from the Presbyterians, who went so far as to describe his proceedings as 'highly mutinous' and 'much diminishing my Lord's honour and the rest of the gentlemen of the army'. Crauford no doubt was going too far in alleging that 'Cromwell and his creatures did nothing but foment sedition and dissension in my Lord's army of horse, . . . to withdraw the hearts of people from the Earl', but it is clear that he was not blameless in this quarrel between Presbyterian and Independent—a quarrel which bade fair to be the undoing of the Parliamentarian cause.

If Crauford had no illusions as to Cromwell's personal enmity, there were Royalists too who now saw in him their most relentless opponent. About this time that subtle prelate John Williams, Archbishop of York, told the King that Oliver 'was the most dangerous enemy his Majesty had. For tho' he were at that time of mean rank and use among them, yet he would climb higher.' The Archbishop, formerly Bishop of Lincoln, had known Cromwell before 1637, 'but never knew his religion. He was a common spokesman for sectaries, and maintained their part with stubbornness. He never discoursed as if he were pleased with your Majesty, and your great officers; and indeed he loves none, that are more than his equals.' The worldly Archbishop recommended 'that either you would win him to you by promises of fair treatment, or catch him by some strategem, and cut him short'. Beyond question friend and foe alike were coming to appreciate Cromwell as a formidable personality. He was, moreover, very much a law unto himself. When Prince Rupert marched from Shrewsbury to raise the siege of Newark it was suggested that if he would march there with 1,500 of his horse he 'would spoil Prince Rupert's market'. To this Oliver replied that 'Sir John Meldrum and the rest would take the town for all the Prince'. An officer answered: 'It is as cheap for our horse to march as to lie still in the stables', which angered Cromwell, who bade him hold his tongue. So far from taking Newark, Meldrum was hemmed in on the banks of the Trent and compelled to surrender to the Prince with all his army. It was a disaster which Cromwell, seventy-nine miles away at Cambridge, might perhaps have prevented. At least he could have tried. One is left wondering what his motivation may have been. Perhaps Meldrum, an old Scots professional soldier, was, like most of his countrymen in the Parliament service, a Presbyterian.

During the early months of 1644 Cromwell's cavalry saw little action. Manchester's infantry stormed Lincoln on 6 May, but horse have little to do in sieges, and all we know is that the Cathedral was severely damaged by 'Cromwell's barbarous crew of Brownists', as the Royalist newspaper *Mercurius Aulicus* styled them. Well disciplined though they were in most respects, Cromwell's troopers could seldom resist their taste for kirkrapine.

In June Manchester marched his army to join Lord Fairfax and the Scots in the siege of York. 'If York be lost I shall esteem my crown little less,' wrote King Charles to his nephew, and on 1 July the Prince by a brilliant manœuvre relieved the city. Instead of biding his time and letting the enemy armies drift apart Rupert must needs offer them battle, though outnumbered by three to two. The outcome was the disaster of Marston Moor (2 July), which spelt ruin for the Royalist cause in the North.

Before the battle began the Prince interrogated a prisoner. One of the questions he asked was: 'Is Cromwell there?'—evidence, were any needed, that now Hampton and Pym were dead, Oliver was emerging as the real leader of the Parliamentarian party.

In the first charge Cromwell was slightly wounded in the neck, probably by a Cavalier colonel, Marcus Trevor. This did not prevent him rallying his men ready for further action. At this juncture Cromwell's colleague and enemy, Major-General Crauford, came raging up, cursing the cavalry for poltroons because they were standing idle. It seems he had not noticed Cromwell, who now intervened saying that he had been wounded. Crauford apologized and temporarily assumed command of the horse, while their leader withdrew to have his wound dressed.

17. *Report from Oliver Cromwell, 1645* (Mansell Collection)

Sr. beinge Comanded by you to this
seruice, I thinke my selfe bound to ac:
quaint you with the good hand of God
towards you, and vs. Wee marched yesterday
after the Kinge whoe went before vs
from Dauentree to Haurebrowe, and quar
tered about six miles from him, this day
wee marched towards him, Hee drew out
to meete vs. both Armies engaged, wee.
after 3 howers fight, very doubtfull
att last routed his Armie, killed and
tooke about 5000. very many officers
but of what quallitye wee yett know
not, wee tooke alsoe about 200. carrag:
all hee had, and all his gunns, beinge
12. in number, whereof 2. were Demi
canon, 2 demie Culueringes, and (I
thinke) the rest Sacers, wee pursued
enimie from three miles short of Ha:
to nine beyond, euen to sight of Leic
whether the Kinge fled. Sr. this is non
other but the hand of God, and to him
aloane belongs the Glorie, wherein no
are to share with him. The Generall
serued you with all faythfullnesse an
honor, and the best comendations I can
giue him is, that I dare say Hee

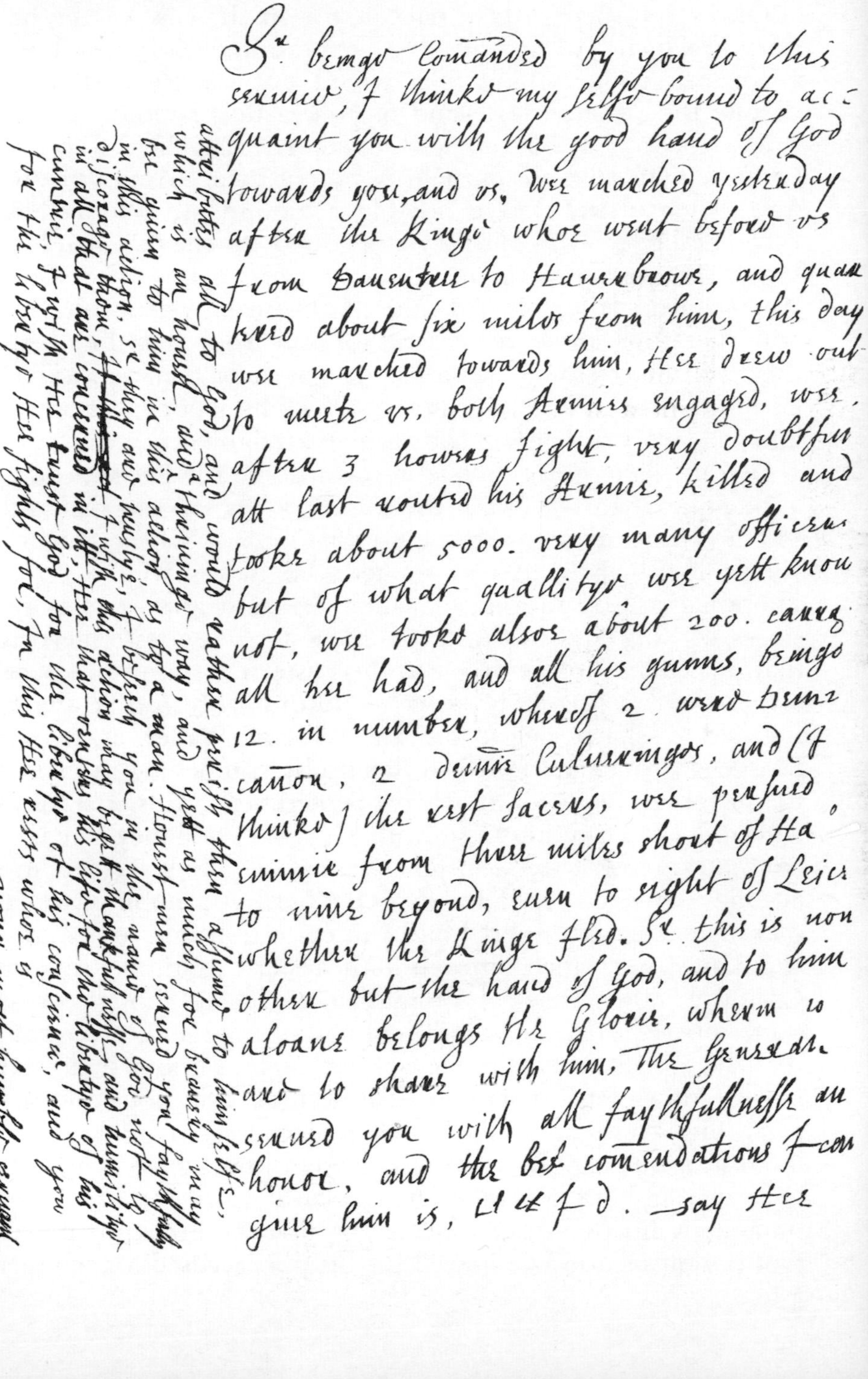

attributes all to God, and would rather perish then assume to himselfe,
which is an honest, and a thriuinge way, and yett as much for brauery may
bee giuen to him in this action as to a man. Honest men serued you faythfully
in this action. Sr they are trustye, I beseech you in the name of God not to
discorage them, I wish this action may beget thankfullnesse and humilitye
in all that are concerned in it, hee that venters his life for the libertye of his
countrie, I wish hee trust God for the libertye of his conscience, and you
for the libertye hee fights for, In this hee rests whoe is

Your most humble seruant
Oliver Cromwell

June 14th 1645.
Hauerbrow

Oliver returned to take part in the final phase of the battle, during which Fairfax and he first routed Goring's hitherto victorious troopers, and then wiped out the Royalist infantry, despite the resolute last stand of Newcastle's famous whitecoats.

Marston Moor was no walk-over. The Cavaliers who fought Cromwell's wing were likened by one of their enemies to an iron wall. Their defeat was a notable achievement. 'Major-General David Leslie seeing us pluck a victory out of the enemies' hands, professed Europe had no better soldiers,' wrote Scoutmaster-General Watson. Rupert for his part said: 'I am sure my men fought well, and therefore know no reason of our rout but this, because the devil did help his servants.' It was now that he nicknamed Cromwell 'Ironsides', the name by which his troopers also became known. Two years of war had forged a magnificent weapon.

Despite their great victory it was to take the Parliamentarians another two years to finish the war. Strategy was not their strong suit and instead of marching south to try conclusions with the King's main army they contented themselves with a series of 'mopping up' operations, of which the most important were the sieges of York and Newcastle. Manchester, even less enterprising than his colleagues, returned to the Eastern Association where his army spent a singularly peaceful autumn. Meanwhile the King inflicted a sharp defeat on Sir William Waller at Cropredy Bridge (29 June) and followed this up by compelling Essex's army to surrender at Lostwithiel (2 September). This last disaster galvanized the Committee of Both Kingdoms and they managed to concentrate some 17,500 men against the King's 9,000 in the Second Battle of Newbury (27 October). An ambitious tactical plan, aimed at assaulting the Royalist position from east and west simultaneously, failed through Manchester's mistiming his attack. Cromwell's own attack was foiled when Goring, though seriously outnumbered, made a magnificent countercharge. The upshot was that the King's army slipped away by night. Furious quarrels followed. Manchester described Cromwell as 'a factious and somewhat inert officer'. Baillie, a Scot, declared: 'It's like, for the interest of our nation, we must crave reason of that darling of the sectaries, and, in obtaining his removal from the army, which himself by his over-rashness has procured, to break the power of that potent faction.' Cromwell for his part accused Manchester of

desiring to bring the war to an end on terms since 'it might be dis-
advantageous to bring the King too low'.

Essex and others met the Scottish Commissioners on 3
December and actually discussed the question whether to accuse
Cromwell under a clause of the Solemn League and Covenant by
which anyone who divided the two kingdoms could be brought to
trial. The lawyer Maynard prevented this, warning them that
Oliver had 'great favour and interest' not only with the Commons
but with some of the Lords, and 'therefore there must be
proofs, . . . to prevail with the Parliament to adjudge him to be an
incendiary'. Next day Cromwell, warned no doubt by Maynard or
some other who had attended this meeting, made a long speech
denying every charge against himself and attacking his superior
officer, Manchester. He had the sense, however, to see that the
quarrel must not be allowed to develop into a straight fight between
Lords and Commons, and, with considerable political skill, he
now shifted his ground, abandoning the attack on Manchester and
laying bare the general misconduct of the war. In a great speech
(9 December) he paved the way for the formation of the New
Model Army, that 'company of poor ignorant men' that was to
win the war.

> It is now the time to speak, or forever hold the tongue. The im-
> portant occasion now is no less than to save a nation out of a
> bleeding, nay almost dying, condition, . . . casting off all lingering
> proceedings, like those of soldiers of fortune beyond the sea, to
> spin out a war. . . .

He claimed that on all sides men were saying that:

> . . . the Members of both Houses have got great places and com-
> mands, and the sword into their hands; and . . . will perpetually
> continue themselves in grandeur, and not permit the War speedily
> to end, lest their own power should determine with it. . . . I know
> the worth of those commanders, Members of both Houses, who are
> yet in power. But, if I may speak my conscience without reflection
> upon any, I do conceive if the Army be not put into another
> method, and the War more vigorously prosecuted, the people can
> bear the War no longer, and will enforce you to a dishonourable
> peace.
> But this I would recommend to your prudence—not to insist

c—c

upon any complaint or oversight of any Commander-in-Chief . . . for as I must acknowledge myself guilty of oversight, so I know they can rarely be avoided in military matters. . . . And I hope we have such true English hearts and zealous affection towards the general weal of our Mother Country as no Member of either House will scruple to deny themselves, and their own private interests, for the public good. . . .

The New Model Army* was commanded by Sir Thomas Fairfax with Cromwell as his second-in-command. The Ironsides now split up and became the two regiments of Sir Thomas Fairfax and Colonel Edward Whalley.

The choice of Fairfax as General rather than Cromwell need surprise nobody. The former was a professional soldier who had done wonders in the North, holding out with a very small army against the formidable army of the Earl of Newcastle. A man of few words, he was a splendid commander in battle, and his fighting record was even more distinguished than that of his second-in-command whose great victories still lay in the future, and to one at least of his contemporaries, that excellent tactician Sir William Waller, Cromwell seemed somewhat unimpressive at this period. Doubtless his failure at Second Newbury, where he was under Waller, prejudiced the latter to some extent. He wrote some years later:

> I cannot but mention the wonder which I have oft times had to see this eagle in his eirey; he at this time, had never shown extraordinary parts; nor do I think he did himself believe that he had them; . . . As an officer he was obedient, and did never dispute my orders, nor argue upon them. He did indeed seem to have great cunning; and whilst he was cautious of his own words . . . he made others talk, until he had, as it were sifted them, and known their most intimate designs.

However that may be, Cromwell was gaining in experience all the time. While he was with Waller he took part in one of those nocturnal raids which earned the former the nickname of 'the Night Owl'. This was on 10 April when they practically destroyed

---

*The New Model Army, formed from those of Essex, Manchester and Waller, consisted of eleven regiments of horse, each 600 strong; a regiment of 1,000 dragoons; and twelve regiments of foot, each of 1,200: total 22,000. There were sufficient men available to bring the cavalry up to strength, but only enough foot to fill half the establishment: the rest were pressed men.

18. *Sir Thomas Fairfax* (Mansell Collection)

His
Excellencie
Thomas Fairfax K.
enerall of the forces
raised by the
Parliament.

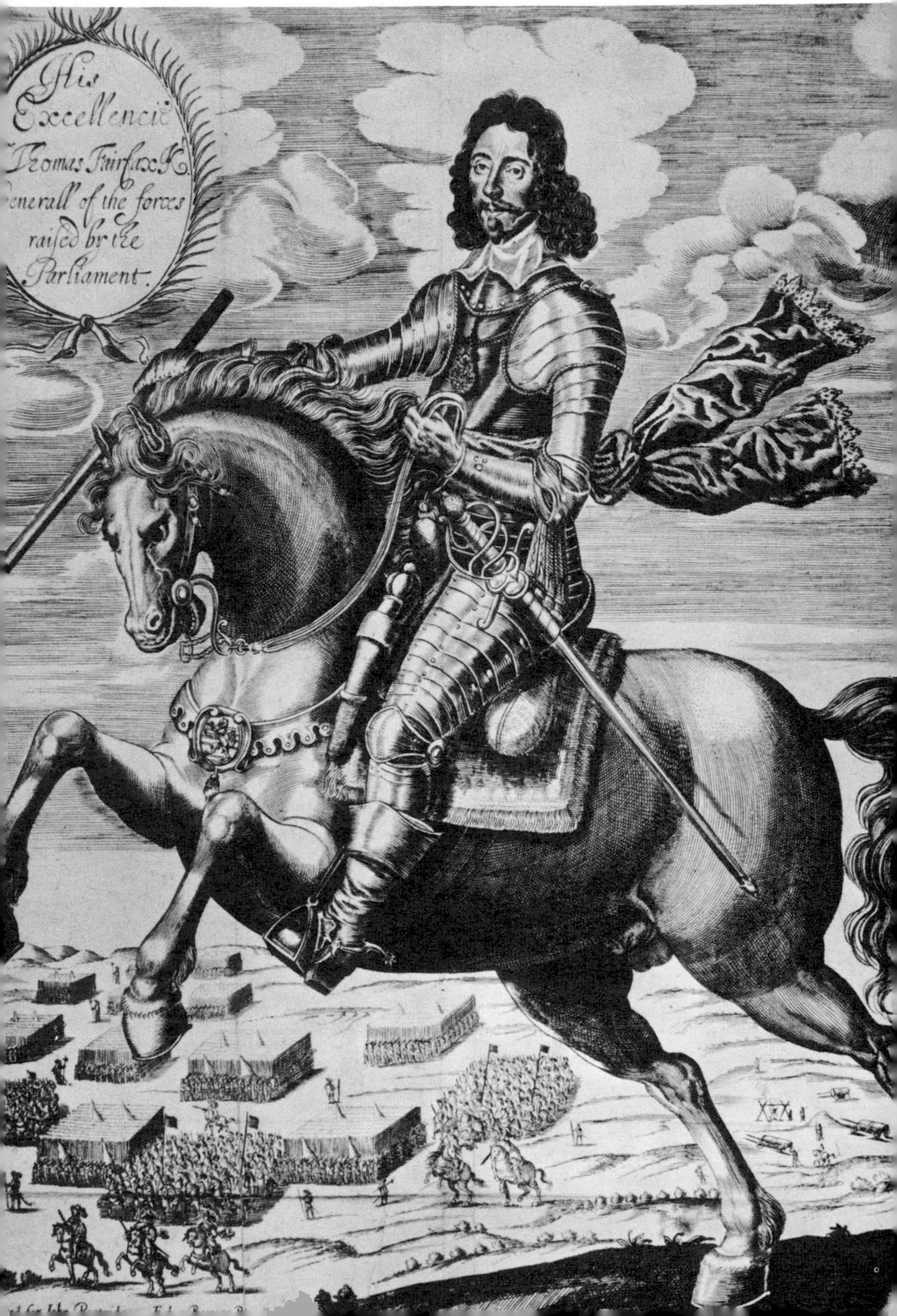

General FAIRFAX with
his FORCES before the City of
OXFORD

Colonel James Long's regiment in its quarters near Lavington in Wiltshire. It may have been this experience that inspired Oliver to carry out his famous Islip raid when in the last week of April he rode through the King's quarters around Oxford, leaving a trail of destruction behind him. Only at Faringdon Castle, which he somewhat rashly attempted to carry by escalade, did he meet with a repulse.

By the Self-Denying Ordinance (10 May), Cromwell, as a member of Parliament, should have laid down his commission, but Fairfax and his Council of War petitioned Parliament (10 June) to make him Lieutenant-General of the New Model, paying him a handsome tribute in so doing.

> The general esteem and affection which he hath both with the officers and soldiers of this whole army, his own personal worth and ability for the employment, his great care, diligence, courage, and faithfulness . . . constant presence and blessing of God that have accompanied him, make us look upon it as the duty we owe to you and the public, to make it our suit.

When three days later on the eve of Naseby Oliver rode into Fairfax's camp, his arrival had an instant effect on the morale of the soldiery. He was received 'with a mighty shout', and cries of 'Ironsides is come to head us'.

In the ensuing battle, it fell to his lot to marshal the cavalry. He was confident of victory: 'I could not (riding alone about my business) but smile out to God in praises, in assurance of victory, because God would, by things that are not, bring to naught things that are . . .'—and, whether from *joie de combattre* or merely excitement, just before the battle began he was seized with a fit of laughter.

Cromwell took command of the right wing, where he had to deal with the Northern Horse under that dour Yorkshireman, Sir Marmaduke Langdale. The Ironsides outnumbered their opponents by almost two to one and made short work of them. Cromwell had his men well in hand and, sending part of them to check the remaining Royalist horse, wheeled the rest against their foot, who resisted with great resolution but in vain.

Once more Cromwell's control and the disciplined valour of his men had turned the tide of battle, for Rupert had routed the

20. *Battle of Naseby, by Cattermole* (Radio Times Hulton Picture Library)

Roundhead left while Astley had thrown their infantry into confusion.

Naseby was the decisive battle of the First Civil War, but Cromwell was to see a good deal more action before it was over. At Bridgwater, which fell on 23 July, Mrs Wyndham, the Governor's wife, came near to ending his career with a cannon shot which struck down an officer at his side. Later she sent a trumpeter to ask if he had received her 'love token'.

In October he had a taste of independent command when Fairfax sent him to clear his communications with London. He took Winchester for the loss of less than a dozen men, stormed and sacked Basing House, where the Marquis of Winchester made a notable defence, and went on to take Langford House in Wiltshire. Siege warfare was very much a feature of the Civil Wars and this was all valuable experience.

During the Second Civil War (1648) Fairfax was engaged in Kent and at the siege of Colchester, so once more Oliver found himself with an independent command. He had first to conduct the siege of Pembroke, which, being inadequately provided with artillery, he reduced by starvation. His next task was to engage the Duke of Hamilton, who had crossed the border with 10,000 Scots and with the support of Northern Cavaliers under Langdale and Sir Philip Musgrave was advancing down the western invasion route. Once Pembroke fell Cromwell moved fast. His men, though unpaid for months, backed him up nobly, marching the 260 miles to Pontefract in twenty-seven days. At Leicester, Oliver managed to procure them new shoes and stockings, an attention to administrative detail that reminds one of Marlborough's preparations for his famous march to the Danube (1704).

The Royalists had managed to seize the castles of Pontefract and Scarborough, and after detaching men to mask these strongholds, Cromwell could only muster some 9,000 men, of whom a third were horse. Nevertheless it was according to one of its officers, Captain John Hodgson, a 'fine smart army, fit for action'.

The Scots on the other hand were neither trained nor had they a proper train of artillery. Hamilton ought to have attempted the relief of the Yorkshire fortresses but instead pushed on towards Preston. With true soldierly instinct Cromwell sought him out, determined to bring on a decisive battle. 'Upon deliberate advice

we chose . . . to put ourselves between their army and Scotland.' In the fighting that followed, Langdale fought with his customary tenacity, but Hamilton had got his men strung out over some fifty miles and allowed his various detachments to get beaten in detail. Cromwell was lucky to be up against such an indifferent general, but nevertheless Preston with the relentless pursuit that followed was a fine feat of arms.

The Irish campaign of 1649–50 adds little to Cromwell's reputation either as a soldier or as a man. The storming of Drogheda at the third assault shows the determination of his followers, though the hideous atrocities that followed reveal a deliberate savagery which did credit neither to them nor their commander, who wrote: '. . . being in the heat of action, I forbade them to spare any that were in arms in the town, and I think that night they put to the sword about 2,000 men.' The great Duke of Wellington thought that: 'The practice of refusing quarter to a garrison which stands an assault is not a useless effusion of blood.' It was accepted that once a breach had been made the defenders ought to surrender, and it is in this light that we must judge Cromwell's actions at Drogheda and Wexford.

However, atrocities in war have a way of boomeranging, and if the strongholds of Trim and Dundalk were abandoned by their terrified garrisons, those of Waterford and Clonmel held out with the courage of desperation. At the last named, Hugh O'Neill, 'an old, surly Spanish soldier', repulsed the Ironsides with a loss of 2,000 men, a defeat which Ireton described as 'the heaviest we ever endured either in England or here'. Adding insult to injury the skilful Governor, his ammunition well-nigh spent, led out his garrison by night and made his way to Waterford, which does not say much for Oliver's vigilance.

Cromwell's campaign in Scotland (1650) began badly, when he found his former ally, David Leslie, impregnably entrenched in lines covering Edinburgh and Leith. After a month's fruitless skirmishing, Cromwell was compelled to withdraw his 'poor, shattered, hungry, discouraged army' to Dunbar, where he found himself trapped. The Scots ensconced on the Lammermuirs blocked Cockburnspath and cut him off from Berwick. 'He [Leslie] lieth so upon the hills that we know not how to come that way without great difficulty; and our lying here daily consumeth our men, who fall sick beyond imagination.' But now when the game was in his hand Leslie must needs move. Cromwell tells us how on the eve of the battle: '. . . the enemy drew down to their right wing about two-thirds of their left wing of horse, . . . shogging also their foot and train much to the right, causing their right wing of horse to edge down towards the sea. We could not well imagine but that the enemy intended to attempt upon us, or to place themselves in a more exact condition of interposition.' He and Lambert watched all this from the Earl of Roxburgh's House, 'and observing this posture, I told him I thought it did give us an opportunity and advantage to attempt upon the enemy, to which he immediately replied, that he had thought to have said the same thing to me. . . .' For all their eight years' service the generals were not too proud to call for an expert opinion. They sent for Colonel George Monck, who had been a professional soldier all his adult life, 'and showed him the thing; and coming to our quarters at night, and demonstrating our apprehensions to some of the colonels, they also cheerfully concurred'.

What had they seen? What was this tactical advantage which Leslie had handed them so obligingly? It was simply that they had only to beat Leslie's right wing to throw his whole army into disorder. In addition they had noticed that the gaps between the Scots cavalry squadrons were too big. Moreover, the English gunners would 'have fair play' at Leslie's left wing while Cromwell's main body was engaging his right.

Cromwell spent an anxious night riding up and down by torchlight to marshal his men and 'biting his lips till the blood ran down his chin without his perceiving it, his thoughts being busily employed to be ready for the action now in hand'. With only 11,000 men against Leslie's 22,000, he had grounds for anxiety.

Zero hour was meant to be daybreak—sunrise was at 5.35 a.m.—but, due to various delays, it was not until 6.00 a.m. that the Ironsides crossed the start line. Even so, Cromwell evidently felt that things were going well, and in the same mood of semi-mystical elation that had sustained him at Naseby 'carried on with a divine impulse. He did laugh so excessively as if he had been drunk, and his eyes sparkled with spirits. "Now let God arise, and his enemies shall be scattered,"* quoth he.'

* Psalm 68.

39

Everything went according to plan—a most unusual thing in war —and after no more than an hour's fighting the Scots were routed, and Oliver and his men were singing Psalm 117 on Doon Hill.

Dunbar and the subsequent capture of Edinburgh did not put an end to Scots resistance, simply because Cromwell had not enough men to hold down the country and to deal with Leslie. By the summer of 1651 this simple truth was evident and in order to break the strategic deadlock Cromwell devised a real masterstroke.

Leslie was near Stirling when, after his victory at Inverkeithing (20 July), Cromwell cut his communications with Perth whilst at the same time opening the road into England. Leslie and King Charles II accepted the invitation and fell into the trap. Once in England Cromwell could make use of local garrisons and of militia. Although some 2,000 English Cavaliers joined the King, the invaders, cornered at Worcester, could only pit 12,000 men against some 28,000 concentrated by Cromwell.

The main tactical feature of Worcester, Cromwell's last fight, his 'crowning mercy', was his bold and imaginative use of a bridge of boats for shifting troops from one bank of the Severn to the other. King Charles II in his second battle* showed a resolute spirit and his counter-attack against Red Hill was well conceived. But Dunbar had broken David Leslie's spirit and as he refused to launch his cavalry the day was lost. Oliver, though not a man-at-arms of Rupert's calibre, gave proof, were any needed, of his personal courage. 'My Lord General did exceedingly hazard himself, riding up and down in the midst of the shot and riding himself to the enemies' foot, offering them quarter, whereto they returned no answer but shot.'

So ended Cromwell's military career, though as head of state he was to be responsible for the higher strategy of his war against the Dutch, and must bear some of the responsibility for the misfortunes of Venables' ill-fated expedition to Hispaniola.

As a soldier Cromwell was hardly in the class of Marlborough and Wellington, of Slim and Montgomery; but his career and his writings give evidence of real strategic as well as tactical skill, of administrative talent and above all of a flair for 'personnel selection'. In nine years' service he was only foiled four times: by Goring at Second Newbury; by Lieutenant-Colonel Roger Burges

* He had been at Edgehill as a boy of twelve.

at Faringdon Castle; at Waterford; and lastly by Hugh O'Neill at Clonmel. But war is full of ups and downs and the commander who has never had a setback has seen but little service. With Gainsborough, Preston, Dunbar and Worcester behind him, the

Protector could look back upon his military career with pride and satisfaction, but, as he himself wrote of Fairfax after Naseby, 'I dare say he attributes all to God.'

I do not ask to see the distant scene,
One step enough for me.
CARDINAL J. H. NEWMAN

\*　　\*　　\*

I tell you we will cut off his head, with the crown on it.
OLIVER CROMWELL

*Part 3*

# The Executioner

26. *The reverse of the Lord Protector Medal, by Thomas Simon, 1653* (National Portrait Gallery)

The New Model Army won the First Civil War for Parliament. The Self-Denying Ordinance which deprived members of their military commands was a logical move and a necessary one. But it was not in human nature for those compelled to give up their commissions to accept this affront without some rankling seeds of discontent. The fact that Cromwell himself had soldiered on cannot have passed without comment. The Parliamentarian party had always consisted of two main elements—the Presbyterians and the Independents. By 1645 the situation was that the former controlled the House and the latter the Army. Thus a gulf grew between the two, so that Sir Philip Stapleton could even speak of the New Model as 'that evil army'. In 1646 the numbers in the House were 'recruited' by new members brought in to fill the places of ejected Royalists and other casualties. The recruits included a number of officers,

*Charles I, from the painting by Van Dyck.* (National Gallery, London).

General Ireton, from the painting by Robert Walker. *(Cromwell Museum, Huntingdon)*

Fairfax, Ireton and Fleetwood among them—all Independents. So once again there were many members who held military rank, but since the war was over the Self-Denying Ordinance had lost its significance. The arrival of these new members gave the Army a voice in Parliament but no more, for the Presbyterians were still decidedly in the ascendant.

Crisis came in March 1647 when Parliament decided to reduce the Army. All would have been well had there been pay for the soldiers' arrears, at a time when the foot had received none for eighteen weeks and the horse none for forty-three! But Parliament had just given the Scots £400,000 (January) to induce them to go home—receiving in return their prisoner and King, Charles.

It was neither honest nor realistic of Parliament to expect regiments to disband *before* they were paid, and the best course would certainly have been to raise the money somehow, or to keep those regiments they could not pay in being. Cromwell for his part, so far from opposing the policy of his colleagues, proposed a practical solution, which was that he should lead a contingent of his veterans to take service under the Calvinist Elector Palatine. Despite serious negotiations, however, this project came to nought.

At first Cromwell was evidently convinced that the soldiers would lay down their arms whenever the House should command them to, but the crisis dragged on and in May he was sent on a commission to examine the grievances of the soldiers. He endeavoured to point out that if Parliament's 'authority falls to nothing, nothing can follow but confusion' (16 May). The commissioners reported that the Army was labouring 'under a deep sense of some suffering', but Cromwell still thought that although the men would not go to Ireland, they would at least disband quietly. In this he may inadvertently have misled the House. At any rate on 27 May Parliament insisted on immediate disbandment and, though prepared to redress minor grievances, still failed to settle the major issue, that of arrears. It was determined that the regiments should be disbanded separately in their various quarters, and that Fairfax's own regiment should be the first to go. Whether this was intended as a gratuitous insult to the general does not appear.

The Army, not to be snared so easily, countered by concentrating at Newmarket and the crisis came to a head. Parliament,

c—d

45

confident of the support of the London Trained Bands, determined to call in the Scots, as if such a coalition could hold the men who had destroyed the King's veteran armies at Naseby and Langport.

Cromwell was now faced by a singularly difficult decision. Was he for Parliament—without whose authority 'nothing can follow but confusion'—or the men, who had fought so nobly for him and were now being wronged? Though never quick to make up his mind in political affairs, four years of soldiering had given him the power to take military decisions. And it was in truth a military decision that had to be taken, for Parliament, by incurring the hostility of its own soldiery, was handing the King a golden opportunity to split his enemies.

In 1646, presumably so that he could attend to his parliamentary duties more easily, Cromwell had moved from Ely to a house in Drury Lane. This was the rendezvous for the secret meetings at which it was determined (31 May) that Cornet George Joyce of Fairfax's Lifeguard should first seize the Train of Artillery at Oxford and then secure the King at Holmby, an object which was achieved on 2 June. Oddly enough Cromwell, though he had clearly taken a leading part in the deliberations of the Army leaders and risked being sent to the Tower, did not set out for Newmarket until the following day (3 June). Perhaps we should take this as proof of his iron nerve. Maybe he braved the danger because he did not wish to show his hand until Joyce had had time to act. Possibly he lingered in London in the vain hope, even at the eleventh hour, of acting as a mediator between Parliament and Army, for though he had now thrown in his lot with the latter, he still attempted to exercise a moderating influence. The inarticulate Fairfax was more of a hand in a fight than in the Council of War, or the General Council of generals, officers and privates, which was chosen to negotiate with Parliament. Thus the eloquent Cromwell was compelled, as second-in-command, to take the lead.

Uncertainty and the defiance of Parliamentary authority implicit in the concentration at Newmarket, and Joyce's coup, could have destroyed discipline. But thanks to Cromwell this did not occur, because as Lilburne put it (July), by his 'unjust subtlety and shifting tricks', he robbed 'the honest and gallant Agitators of all their power and authority, and solely placed it in a thing called a council of war'. Having regained control of the Army, Cromwell still hoped for a reasonable settlement. He was a signatory of a letter to the City of London, which indeed he may have drafted, in which he set forth the soldiers' viewpoint.

> As Englishmen—and surely our being soldiers hath not stripped us of that interest, . . . we desire a settlement of the peace of the Kingdom and of the liberties of the subject, . . . which before we took arms, were by the Parliament used as arguments to invite us and divers of our dear friends out; some of whom have lost their lives in this War.

As time went by the Army became more demanding, and the Declaration of 14 June, drafted by Ireton, sought the purging of Parliament, the proscription of eleven members, including Denzil Holles—one of the famous five members of 1642—and a new House. Cromwell, while protesting his desire 'to maintain the authority of Parliament', nevertheless signed the Declaration.

Negotiations followed during which Cromwell succeeded in calming the fire-eating Agitators, who were for a march on London: 'Whatsoever we get by a treaty will be firm and durable. . . . That you have by force I look upon it as nothing' (16 July). Ireton and Lambert now drafted the famous document known as the 'Heads of the Proposals', which was intended as the basis for a settlement between King, Parliament and Army. At this juncture their opponents gave up the struggle. Eight of the few remaining Peers and fifty-seven of the Commons, declaring that Parliament, threatened by the violence of the London mob, was no longer free, took refuge with the Army. Though the Presbyterians attempted to resist with the militia of London, their efforts were in vain. On 6 August the Army entered London without opposition and Holles and his supporters fled.

The Army, having failed to make peace with its employers, now sought a settlement with its erstwhile enemy, the King. Nor were the terms outlined in the Heads of the Proposals unreasonable. The Cavaliers were not to be ruined by sequestration; there was to be religious toleration for all and the King, though his power was controlled by Parliament, was to be restored. This last point was no doubt at the root of Charles's rejection of the terms, though mere dislike of Fairfax and Cromwell may have been the overriding factor. The one he styled their 'brutish general', and

the other's record as a despoiler of cathedrals, as the man who sacked Basing and, simply, as 'Ironsides', was all too well known to him. Before new terms could be offered, the King, prompted by the Scottish envoys, had fled to the Isle of Wight. Some think that, persuaded that the soldiers were out of hand, he feared murder. Marvell's famous lines enshrine a traditional view that Cromwell baited him into this precipitate flight:

> Twining subtle fears with hope,
> He wove a net of such a scope,
> That Charles himself might chase
> To Carisbrook's narrow case,
> That thence the royal actor borne
> The tragic scaffold might adorn.

But though in the war he had said 'if the King were before me I would shoot him as another', it is doubtful in fact whether the idea of the King's execution had as yet entered the murky depths of Oliver's mind. Yet this cannot be certain, for already Strafford and Laud had perished on the block and Cromwell was by no means incapable of imagining that the path the ministers had trod might be followed by their master.

Irritated by Royalist rumours—widely believed—that his price for a restoration of the King was the Garter and an earldom, Cromwell realized that in hoping to make a treaty with the King he had been wasting time. The soldiers too were becoming ever more impatient and mutinous. Firm action by Fairfax and Cromwell restored order, though not without the execution of a corporal, shot at the head of Colonel Robert Lilburne's regiment.

In January Charles rejected four bills which, together, amounted to Parliament's ultimatum. If his hope was to play off his opponents against each other, he had merely succeeded in bringing them together, agreed at least that the people could no longer 'expect safety and government from an obstinate man whose heart God had hardened'. But if the King had failed to widen the rift between Parliament and Army he could at least congratulate himself on engineering a fatal breach between his English and Scots subjects. For Parliament, not content with voting that no further addresses should be made to the King, now excluded the representatives of Scotland from the Committee of Both Kingdoms. On

26 December the King and the Scottish Commissioners concluded the secret alliance of Scots and Royalists known as 'the Engagement'.

The year 1647 had been thoroughly unsatisfactory. No settlement had been achieved and both the power of Parliament and the discipline of the Army had been undermined. Parliament, saved by a hair's breadth from an armed clash with its own soldiery, had now come to a point where war with Scotland was inevitable. And Cromwell, though unquestionably the most powerful man in the Kingdom, had added to the numbers of his enemies, who now included not only the Cavaliers and the Presbyterians, but even men like John Lilburne, who, speaking at the bar of the House, accused him of underhand dealings with Charles—'those cursed carnal conferences with the King' as the Army leaders called them when they held their great prayer-meeting at Windsor in April.

By this time war had broken out in South Wales; the Cavaliers had seized Carlisle and Berwick and a Scots army was raising. In this atmosphere army leaders declared that 'it was their duty, if ever the Lord brought them back in peace, to call Charles Stuart, that man of blood, to account for all the blood he had shed and the mischief he had done to his utmost, against the Lord's cause and people in these poor nations'. In the months while he was besieging Pembroke Castle, marching to Preston and lingering before Pontefract Cromwell had time enough to ponder the significance of these words. To him a man like the turncoat Poyer, who led the revolt in Wales, had sinned against the light, while of Cavaliers, like Langdale and Musgrave, he said:

> This, is a more prodigious treason than any other hath been perfected before; because the former quarrel was that Englishmen might rule over one another, this to vassalize us to a foreign nation [the Scots]. And their fault that appeared in this summers' business is certainly double to theirs who were in the first, because it is the repetition of the same offence against all the witnesses that God hath borne.

Thus Oliver reasoned, ignoring the occasions—Stratton, Roundway Down and Newark to name a few—when the Lord had chastised his anointed, and averring in effect that Naseby, Langport and Torrington were 'light' enough to show that to oppose Parliament or Army thereafter was simply to magnify the former offence of supporting the old order of things—Mitre and Crown. But if sometimes he put things so simply he seldom saw them thus clearly, and at this stage even less than usual. Holles was back in Westminster and—'an accursed thing'—had actually re-opened negotiations with Charles.

When, on 18 November, Fairfax, on behalf of the Army, demanded that the King as 'the grand author of our troubles' be brought to trial, Oliver was still at Pontefract, doubtless struggling with his conscience as much as the Royalist garrison. Ordered south, he handed over to Lambert—who one would have supposed perfectly capable of conducting a siege whether Cromwell was there or not—and journeyed to London, arriving on the day *after* 'Pride's Purge'. Colonel Pride, prompted no doubt by Oliver's quick-witted son-in-law, Ireton, had arrested forty-five members of Parliament and excluded ninety-six more. Once more the Presbyterians had been driven from the scene, and the trial of the King, contemplated by the army leaders for the last seven months, was now a real possibility.

Though Cromwell had played no part in the Purge he was 'glad of it', and he and Ireton set about their self-imposed task of bringing their King to trial. Though the outcome was foreordained they were at pains to give the proceedings an air of legality. The Rump of the Commons obligingly created a tribunal of 135 Commissioners as judges. Of this formidable array over half had the wit to avoid serving.

To Cromwell, though not in doubt as to the need to bring 'this Man against whom the Lord hath witnessed' to trial, this must have been infuriating, for he was genuinely preoccupied with the legal aspects of the business.

The Commissioners met in the Painted Chamber of the ancient Palace of Westminster. Their first session, which only fifty-three attended, was on 8 January. The first to answer his name was Thomas, Lord Fairfax, the Lord General. Four lawyers were chosen to frame the charge. They included the Dutch scholar Isaac Dorislaus, a former Professor of Ancient History at Cambridge. A bad end was in store for him: he was to be murdered by a band of Royalist soldiers at the Hague in May 1649.

30. TOP: *General Ireton* (Mansell Collection)

31. BOTTOM: *Lord Fairfax* (Mansell Collection)

BIBL
TA
SACR
A.

MAG
NÀ
CHAR
TA

STA
TV
TES

RE
POR
TES

*Quercu cadente, ligna*
*quivis colligit*

*Infertum Vulgus, mentigrave*

Fatted for Slaughter.

33. *Charles I, after the picture by Lely* (Mansell Collection)

On the morning of 9 January the Sergeant-at-arms, Edward Dendy, attended by six trumpeters and two troops of horse, rode into Westminster Hall, and afterwards to Cheapside and the old Exchange, to proclaim that Charles Stuart, King of England, was to be tried, and that the Court of Justice would be in session from 10 January. No onlooker ventured to protest.

The Commissioners met again on 10 January. This time Fairfax was not among them. No doubt he preferred to busy himself with the daily routine of running his army and to leave the unsavoury business of killing a king to his second-in-command. Henceforth Fairfax, though he saw the King's execution as the murder it was, neither helped nor hindered the proceedings, excusing his inaction by asserting that to protest would have been to split the Army and bring a renewed outbreak of Civil War. Indeed Lady Fairfax was to play a more active part in the trial than her husband, for she intervened twice from her place in the spectators' gallery. On the first occasion, when Fairfax's name was called, she cried out: 'Not here and never will be; he has too much sense.' Later when Bradshaw charged the King of 'treason and other high crimes exhibited against him in the name of the people of England', she caused a tumult by shouting: 'Not half or a quarter of them. Oliver Cromwell is a rogue and a traitor!' She was not alone in asserting the illegality of the proceedings. Algernon Sidney had the courage to tell Cromwell: 'First, the King can be tried by no court; second, no man can be tried by this court.' The truth of both points is incontestable. That Oliver knew it is plain from an episode on 20 January, the day the trial began. The Commissioners waited in the Painted Chamber for the King to arrive. They heard that he was landing at the steps:

At which Cromwell ran to the window, looking on the King as he came up the garden; he turned as white as the wall . . . then turning to the board said thus: 'My masters, he is come, he is come, and now we are on doing that great work that the whole nation will be full of. Therefore I desire you to let us resolve here what answer we shall give the King when he comes before us, for the first question he will ask us will be by what authority and commission we do try him?' For a time no one answered. Then after a little space, Henry Marten rose up and said: 'In the name of the Commons in Parliament assembled and all the good people of England.'

The Commissioners had been selected with some care, ranging from a group of colonels, men of humble birth like Thomas Pride the drayman and John Hewson the cobbler, to Lord Monson, who was not quite right in the head, and creatures of Cromwell such as Sir John Danvers and John Downes. The last was to provoke Oliver's 'scornful wrath' when he refused to consent to the sentence.

To add to Cromwell's troubles Charles played his part with dignity and courage. 'For the charge,' he said, 'I value it not a rush. It is the liberties of the people of England that I stand for. For me to acknowledge a new court that I never heard of before— I that am your King, that should be an example to all the people of England to uphold justice, to maintain the old laws—indeed I do not know how to do it.'

Though the sentence of the court was inevitable, only fifty-nine of the Commissioners were induced to sign the death warrant. Cromwell, anxious to make it appear that the Commissioners who had agreed to the sentence were unanimous, did not hesitate to browbeat the more irresolute, mostly members of the Commons rather than officers of the New Model. On 29 January he stood at the door of the House, intercepting Commissioners as they went in. 'Those that are gone in shall set their hands,' he said, 'I will have their hands now.'

The dawn came up icy cold over the frozen Thames. 'Death is not terrible to me,' the King told an attendant as he was dressing. 'I bless my God I am prepared.' He walked briskly from St James's to Whitehall, and was there kept four hours waiting while the Commons hurried through a bill making it illegal for anyone to proclaim a new King, About two o'clock King Charles was led to the scaffold, where he addressed a few words to the men grouped about him: 'The chief causers of my death, who they are, God knows. . . .' Ireton's part he may not have suspected, but of Cromwell's he can have had no doubt.

Firm in the knowledge that he was 'the Martyr of the people', that he had a good cause and a gracious God, the King laid his head upon the block. The axe fell and from the multitude there rose, as young Philip Henry wrote: 'Such a groan as I never heard before, and desire I may never hear again.'

Dying like a martyr and a gentleman Charles had turned the

35. *Execution of Charles I* (Radio Times Hulton Picture Library)

tables on Oliver. His manifest faults were washed away in his blood. England remembered with sudden shock that she was at heart Royalist. Scotland saw her sovereign slain and prepared for inevitable war.

No Royalist ever struck such a blow for the British Monarchy as did Cromwell on the day that he had his King beheaded.

> I am ready to serve not as a King, but as a constable . . . a good constable to keep the peace of the parish.
>
> OLIVER CROMWELL

*Part 4*

# The Dictator

> A free vote of the people, taken at any time after the execution of Charles I, would have restored the monarchy. But Oliver could not afford to permit such freedom.
>
> H. A. L. FISHER

Cromwell's 'reign', the period of the Commonwealth and the Protectorate, lasted for nine years. Throughout this period he depended for support on the Protestant sectaries who were the backbone of his army. They were men who could win him battles by land and sea, and who could hold down the country by imposing military government. But they could not make Oliver's rule popular. As time went by, and the standing army became increasingly an object of hatred, the opposition to the Protector became ever more widespread. During the last years of his life, when the country groaned under the rule of the Major-Generals (1655–58), his bitter opponents included not only the Royalists and the Presbyterians, but ranged from those who sought the ideal of civilian liberty to those who regretted the simple pleasures suppressed by their grim Puritan masters. Cromwell, who had fought so stoutly for the privileges of Parliament, could never count upon

C–E

37. *Defeat of the Dutch fleet by Admiral Blake, 1652* (Cromwell Museum, Huntingdon)

the support of a House willing to accept unquestioned his anomalous personal position or the religious views of the hard core of his Independent supporters. The champion of liberty and constitutional rule found that his power was too narrow-based to permit him room to manœuvre towards the objective of a genuinely free Parliament. The man who had killed a king could hope for nothing but the bitter hatred of the Cavaliers, who though beaten were still numerous. The 'darling of the sectaries' could not expect his position to be unchallenged by the Presbyterians. The wonder is not that the period of the Interregnum contributed so little to the domestic progress of the people, but that such an unpopular government endured so long. That it did so can partly be attributed to Cromwell's stature as a person, and partly to the vigour and efficiency of his army.

The first two years of Cromwell's personal rule were relatively free from political difficulty, but only because the country was once again at war. The campaigns of Dunbar and Worcester were, of course, the direct consequence of the execution of King Charles, who had, after all, been a Scottish King. But after Worcester, that 'crowning mercy', the English republicans looked to their 'chief of men' to bring about and consolidate the reformation in Church and State for which they had fought so long. It may be that the reluctant dictator did not feel altogether equal to the task. 'I am', he wrote, 'a poor weak creature . . . yet accepted to serve the Lord and his people. Indeed . . . you know not me, my weaknesses, my inordinate passions, my unskilfulness, and everyway unfitness to my work. Yet, the Lord, who will have mercy on whom He will, does as you see.' The Tuscan ambassador could not discover in him 'any ambition save for the public good, to which he brings all his spirit and power'.

The future government of the country, both in Church and State, remained unresolved when in 1652 war broke out between England and the Dutch, and Cromwell's attention naturally became engrossed in its conduct, and the problems of paying for it. In part the cost was met by confiscating the estates of Royalists. This measure, rather surprisingly, provoked Oliver's wrath: 'Poor men were driven like flocks of sheep by forty in a morning to confiscation of goods and estates, without any man being able to give a reason why two of them should forfeit a shilling.' It was not only

that his sense of justice was outraged. He had been hoping, how-ever unreasonably, for 'a settlement with somewhat of monarchial power in it', and had given his opinion that it 'would be very effectual' (December 1651).

The old strife between Parliament and Army was never far below the surface, and usually showed its ugly head when the question of arrears arose. The Army regarded the members as a gang of self-seeking profiteers. It is an attitude that has been not unknown in the forces since that date. Cromwell had real difficulty in keeping his supporters in check, for they were impatient for a dissolution. Urged on by Lambert and Harrison, Cromwell described himself as 'pushed on by two parties to do that, the con-sideration of the issue whereof makes my hair stand on end'.

The crisis came when it was revealed to Cromwell that Vane and Hesilrige were plotting to put a new general in his place, and to adjourn until November. In the meanwhile the country was to be ruled by the Council of State.

On 20 April 1653 occurred one of the most famous scenes the Commons has ever witnessed, when Cromwell rose in his wrath and rebuked his fellow members for 'their injustice, delays of justice, self-interest, and other faults . . . charging them not to have a heart to do anything for public good', and to have 'espoused the corrupt interest of Presbytery and lawyers who were the supporters of tyranny and oppression'. His eloquence waxed as his rage increased. 'Perhaps you think this is not Parliamentary language,' he cried, 'I confess it is not, neither are you to expect any such from me.' With that he put his hat on and began to stride up and down the centre of the Chamber, reproaching individual members as the spirit moved him.

Then he cried out: 'It is not fit that you should sit as a Parlia-ment any longer. You have sat long enough, unless you had done more good.' Sir Peter Wentworth ventured a protest. 'Come, come!' Oliver replied, 'I will put an end to your prating. You are no Parliament. I say you are no Parliament. I will put an end to your sitting.' With that he ordered Harrison to call in the musketeers he had prudently stationed in the lobby beforehand. 'Fetch him down,' Oliver cried, pointing to Speaker Lenthall, the man who had once defied his King and was as ready to resist Cromwell. Algernon Sidney also showed fight. 'Put him out,'

*The Parliamentarian Admiral. Robert Blake* (Radio Times Hulton Picture Library)

40. *Oliver Cromwell refusing the Crown of England* (Mansell Collection)

Cromwell cried. Then, pointing to the mace: 'What shall we do with this bauble? . . . Here, take it away!' As the last of the Rump departed Oliver attempted to justify his action: 'It is you that have forced me to this, for I have sought the Lord night and day, that He would rather slay me than put me upon the doing this work.' He had nothing to fear from them for as he said later there 'was not so much as the barking of a dog or any general and visible repining at it'.

With the dissolution of the Council of State, which followed that afternoon, Cromwell as Commander-in-Chief was, whether he liked it or not, dictator. His reluctance is evident from his desire to replace the Rump with a new Parliament. It was this that led to the so-called Barebones Parliament,* an assembly of 140 Puritan notables, 'men fearing God and hating covetousness'. Welcoming them (4 July 1653) Cromwell said, in a lengthy speech full of Scriptural quotations, that he did not desire 'to grasp at the power' himself nor 'to keep it in military hands, no not for a day'. Never at a loss for an eloquent phrase he told them that they must convince the nation 'that as men fearing God have fought them out of their bondage, so men fearing God do now rule them in the fear of God'. He had designed neither the downfall of the monarchy nor the dissolution of the Rump.

> I never looked to see such a day as this. . . . Indeed it is marvellous, and it hath been unprojected. . . . And indeed this hath been the way God hath dealt with us all along; to keep things from our eyes . . . so that we have seen nothing in all His dispensations long beforehand—which is also a witness, in some measure, to our integrity.

This is a convincing passage, illustrating as it does the difficulty with which he met and surmounted successive political problems —problems so much more complex than the quick decisions of the battlefield.

The Barebones Parliament proved a fanatical crew, full of Anabaptists and Fifth Monarchy Men. Cromwell was far too moderate for the taste of the majority. Since he was still in favour of a State Church there were Independents who looked upon him as 'the Man of Sin' and, more picturesquely, 'the Old Dragon'. Men like

* Thomas ('Praise-God') Barbon was one of its members.

41. *Major-General Lambert* (Radio Times Hulton Picture Library)

this hoped to oust Cromwell and make Harrison General in his place.

> The Lord begins to honour us,
> The Saints are marching on,
> The sword is sharp, the arrows swift
> To destroy Babylon.

In this crisis Cromwell found an effective ally in the Yorkshire soldier Lambert, who got rid of the Saints by a simple stratagem. On 12 December he and the more moderate members got up early and voted that Parliament should resign its powers into the hands of the Lord General. Two files of musketeers were at hand to disperse those who refused to surrender their seats.

Cromwell denied all foreknowledge of this manœuvre, but it suited him as well as Pride's Purge had done. On the other hand he was no nearer settling his constitutional problems. 'My power was again by this resignation as boundless and unlimited as before, all things being subject to arbitrariness, and myself a person having power over the three nations without bound or limit set. . . .' On 16 December 1653 he accepted the title of Protector.

The first Parliament of the Protectorate was elected in the summer of 1654. In his opening speech Cromwell assured the members that they were a free Parliament. They included at least a hundred former members of the Long Parliament, at least forty Presbyterians and a number of Republicans. There were even a few Royalists from Wales and the West. But there was also a solid body of army officers. A hundred members, including Hesilrige, refused to sign the Engagement to be faithful to the Protector and the Commonwealth and were excluded. This Parliament proved no more successful than its immediate predecessors and on 22 January 1655 Cromwell dissolved it.

Meanwhile he had survived Gerard's assassination plot (May 1654) and his creature, John Thurloe, had given him timely warning of Royalist and Leveller plans for a rising. The Cavaliers were better soldiers than conspirators, and when (11 March 1655) Colonel John Penruddock surprised Salisbury, his success was short-lived. There was no general insurrection, and he and his 400 followers were compelled to surrender at South Molton (14 March). The colonel, though promised quarter, was executed while most of his followers were transported to Barbados.

42. *The Lord Protector, from the painting by Samuel Cooper* (Mansell Collection)

Penruddock's Rising, militarily insignificant as it was, convinced Cromwell that the Royalists were irreconcilable. At a time when he was disbanding 10,000 of his standing army on grounds of economy he was faced with the problem of policing the country. The solution he struck upon was to divide England into eleven districts, each governed by a Major-General. In addition to keeping order these officers were expected to suppress vice of every sort, a duty which they interpreted as the spirit moved them. To police their areas they were provided with troops of horse. To pay for these a Decimation Tax was imposed on all Cavaliers, despite the fact that Cromwell himself had sponsored the Act of Oblivion by which Royalists who had compounded for their estates were free from further impositions.

In the long run the second Parliament of the Protectorate was no more successful than the first. When its second session began (January 1658) there were two chambers, for a new Upper House had been selected. It included seven of Cromwell's family and seventeen regimental commanders! Mrs Hutchinson spoke for the Republicans when she wrote that Cromwell 'took upon himself to make lords and knights, and wanted not many fools, both of army and gentry, to accept of and strut in this mock title'. The elevation of many of his close supporters left the Protector's following in the Lower House seriously thinned. The Republicans were in high hopes of outvoting the Cromwellians and recalling the Long Parliament. Cromwell was not to be caught napping, however. He endured their trouble-making for just over a fortnight and then dissolved Parliament once more. 'And let God be judge between you and me,' he said. 'Amen,' they replied.

Other troubles of every sort beset the Protector's last years. First there was the assassination plot of Miles Sindercombe, the Leveller, who cheated the gallows by poisoning himself in the Tower (13 February 1657). Then there was something like mutiny in his own regiment of horse, due to the troop commanders' 'dislike of the present government'. Though they were 'willing still to continue in the army and follow his Highness upon the grounds of the old cause', they were not willing to say what they meant by that expression. Cromwell dismissed them all, much to the indignation of their commanding officer, Major William Packer, who had thought Cromwell's new Upper House

. . . was not a 'Lords' House, but another House. But for my under-
taking to judge this, I was sent for, accused of perjury, and outed of
a place of £600 per annum. I would not give it up. He told me I
was not apt: I, that had served him fourteen years, ever since he
was captain of a troop of horse . . . and had commanded a regiment seven years; without any trial or appeal, with the breath of
his nostrils I was outed; and lost not only my place, but a dear
friend to boot. Five captains under my command, all of integrity,
courage, and valour, were outed with me. . . .

Certainly it seems a strangely heavy-handed way for an old soldier
to deal with his own regiment and his own comrades-in-arms. But
in an army that had grown up from the old rebel armies of 1642
there must have been undercurrents of mutual distrust and
political intrigue hard for the British soldier of this age to
comprehend.

In May there was an alarm that the Royalists meant to burn the
City. This may well have been 'a put up job' to stir up public
opinion against the Cavaliers at the time of the trial of Sir Henry
Slingsby. Slingsby, who had been trapped ('trepanned') by
Thurloe, with Cromwell's knowledge, in a plot to suborn the
garrison of Hull, was beheaded on 8 June. Dr Hewitt, once
chaplain of Charles I's Lifeguard of foot, and the favourite
preacher of Cromwell's daughter, Elizabeth Claypole, followed
Slingsby to the block despite all her pleas. She died soon after,
probably of cancer, reproaching the Protector for the death of
the King and Dr Hewitt. 'The sense of her outward misery in the
pains she endured, took deep impression upon him, who indeed
ever was a most indulgent and tender Father. . . .' He did not long
survive his favourite daughter, succumbing to 'a bastard tertian
ague' on 3 September, the anniversary of Dunbar and Worcester.
'It is a fearful thing to fall into the hands of the living God,' he
muttered as his end drew near.

The funeral cost £60,000, of which £19,000 was still unpaid in
1659. John Evelyn thought it 'the joyfullest funeral I ever saw, for
there were none that cried but dogs'. He was, of course, a Royalist,
but the fact remains that the English were well content to see the
last of Oliver if it meant release from the arbitrary rule of his
Major-Generals and a return to something like the 'good old days'
before the country had drifted into civil war.

The Protector writes to Sir William Paston of Oxnitt, Norfolk, authorizing the seizure of guns, arms etc., in the neighbourhood. Dated June 14th, 1656.

*(On loan to the Cromwell Museum, Huntingdon by the London Museum).*

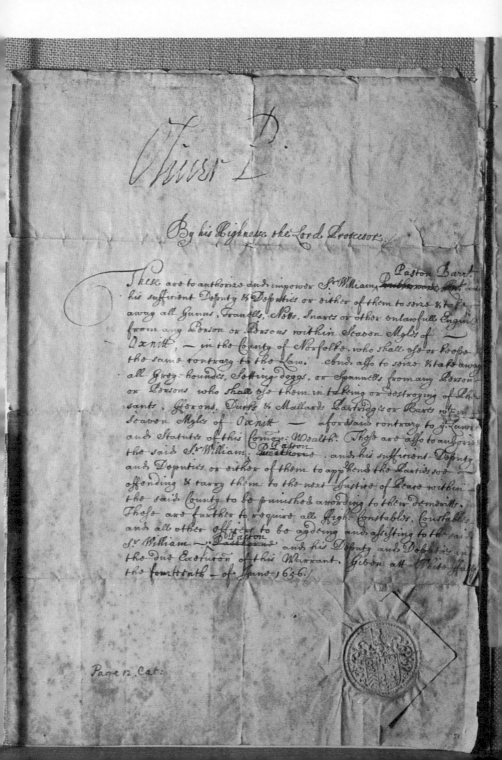

*Oliver P.*

By his Highnesse the Lord Protector.

Paston Barrt.

These are to authorize and impower Sʳ William Paston and his sufficient Deputy & Deputies or either of them to seise & take away all Gunns, Tramells, Netts, Snares or other onlawfull Engins from any Person or Persons within Seaven Myles of Oxnitt, — in the County of Norfolke who shall use or possesse the same contrary to the Law. And also to seise & take away all Grey-houndes, Setting-doggs, or Spannells from any Person or Persons who shall use them in taking or destroying of Pheasants, Herons, Ducks & Mallards Partridges or Hares within Seaven Myles of Oxnitt — aforesaid contrary to the Lawes and Statutes of this Common=Wealth. These are also to authorize the said Sʳ William Paston and his sufficient Deputy and Deputies or either of them to apprehend the Parties soe offending & carry them to the next Justice of Peace within the said County to be punished according to their demeritts. These are further to require all High Constables, Constables and all other Officers to be aydeing and asisting to the said Sʳ William Paston and his Deputy and Deputies in the due Execution of this Warrant. Given att White Hall the fourteenth — of June 1656.

Page 12. Cat.

*Robert Cromwell, from the painting by Robert Walker.* (Cromwell Museum, Huntingdon).

And thou the War and Fortune's son,    March indefatigably on,
And for the last effect    Still keep the sword erect.

ANDREW MARVELL, 1650

*Part 5*

# Fortune's Son

At the outbreak of the First Civil War Cromwell had yet to make his name. He was not one of the most prominent leaders of Pym's party, and was given command not of a regiment but of a troop. Although a member of Parliament of long standing he owed his advancement to military prowess rather than political skill. His successes at Gainsborough, Naseby, Marston Moor and Basing House placed this amateur soldier among the foremost generals of his age, though it is often forgotten that it was Sir Thomas Fairfax, not Cromwell, that commanded the New Model Army. That Cromwell owed his promotion to genuine military talent cannot be denied. He also owed something to the incompetence of some of the other Parliamentarian generals. Had the Earls of Essex and Manchester proved thunderbolts of war there would have been no need for the New Model. His victory at Preston consolidated Cromwell's military reputation at the time when the New Model

was moving towards its final reckoning with the King. Seldom can any army have had at its head a general so inarticulate as Sir Thomas Fairfax and a second-in-command as eloquent as Oliver Cromwell. The latter was bound to take the lead, the more so since Fairfax, who had only been a member of Parliament since 1646, was politically inept. Cromwell on the other hand had been in the forefront of the Parliamentarian leaders for at least four years. By the end of 1644 his military reputation was sufficient to enable him to stand up to the Earl of Manchester in the bitter quarrels at Westminster that followed the second battle of Newbury. His effective intervention in the debate on the Self-

Denying Ordinance is proof that by then he was also a politician of the first importance. But he owed his new standing to the sword.

As a statesman he displayed much of the courage that he had shown in the field, though little of the power of quick decision that had marked him as a soldier. His admirers, misled perhaps by his undoubted eloquence, have overrated his political skill. Once he had brought about the execution of the King he was really in a hopeless position simply because his government lacked the popular support without which, then as now, a government can achieve little beyond mere survival. It was the sword which

46. *Trial of Charles I in Westminster Hall, 1649, from the painting by Fisk* (Radio Times Hulton Picture Library)

brought Cromwell to power and the sword that kept him there. It cannot be sufficiently emphasized that all his subsequent troubles stemmed from the illegal trial and murder of the King, which deprived Cromwell of all hope of uniting the nation behind him. It was worse than a crime: it was a blunder. It can be explained, but never excused. When he determined to bring Charles to the block Cromwell's judgment was clouded by his religious fanaticism. In his eyes the King was 'this Man against whom the Lord hath witnessed'. The triumphs and disasters of war fall, like the rain, on the just and the unjust. Only a zealot could see Marston Moor and Naseby as evidence of divine disapproval of the

47. *St James's Palace, London* (Mansell Collection)

Royalist cause. Yet Cromwell was not the first general nor the last to put it about that he had the Almighty in support—if not under command. 'I beseech you, in the bowels of Christ, think it possible you may be mistaken,' he had once adjured the General Assembly of the Church of Scotland.* The conviction that one's words and actions are 'infallibly agreeable to the Word of God' is a strength and a comfort. It can also be a snare and a delusion.

Though by the standards of the present age Cromwell was a religious fanatic, and although during the war he had permitted his soldiers considerable licence in ravaging the churches of his

* Letter of 3 August 1650.

81

enemies, he was not, for his period, notably intolerant in matters of religion. As evidence of this assertion one may point to his allowing the Jews to settle in England. Still it would be difficult to convince an Irish Catholic that Cromwell's toleration was a plant of strong growth. The followers of Archbishop Laud, too, would be astonished to hear Cromwell described as tolerant. In truth one has to be a Jew, a Quaker or some sectarian to see Oliver in that light.

Cromwell's record in home affairs, fumbling but well-intentioned attempts to establish a free Parliament, leading only to the heavy-handed and incompetent rule of the Major-Generals,

is unimpressive. He had the misfortune that Ireton, the ablest of those he depended upon, died early (1651). To a great extent his advisers were soldiers like Harrison and Lambert, whose political outlook was, if anything, even narrower than his own. Certain of his measures, notably the Decimation Tax, were unjustifiable by any standards.

In foreign affairs, however, he was somewhat more successful. 'What brave things he did and made all the neighbour princes fear him', as Samuel Pepys put it. His alliance with Portugal (1654) gave him the use of Lisbon, and enabled his admiral, Blake, to enter the Mediterranean, and gave a hint of what the world had to

expect from the seapower of England. 'With what prodigious *bravura* did she not make her début in this new rôle, when Blake's fleet, chasing Prince Rupert's privateers, called upon Tuscany and the Pope for indemnities, bombarded Tunis, and showed the flag at Malta and Venice, Toulon and Marseilles!'*

Cromwell would have liked to have based his foreign policy on a league of Protestant powers, but though in the end he resumed the ancient struggle with Spain it was as the ally of Catholic France. Cromwell could hardly be expected to foresee that France rather than Spain was destined to be the chief threat to the balance of power in Europe.

* H. A. L. Fisher: *A History of Europe*, p. 660.

51. *Richard Cromwell, who briefly succeeded his father as Lord Protector* (Mansell Collection)

During the Civil Wars the Dutch had been sympathetic to the Parliamentarian cause, but commercial rivalry and the Stadt-holder's protection of the English royal family brought on the first of the three Anglo-Dutch wars which led to Holland's decline as a world power.

It is certain that in Cromwell's time England cut a figure in the world. It was his 6,000 redcoats that spearheaded the French victory over the Spaniards at Dunkirk Dunes (4 June 1658). His reward was the fortresses of Mardyke and Dunkirk, 'a bridle to the Dutch, and a door into the continent', as Thurloe put it.

On the whole it seems that Cromwell handled foreign policy

52. *General George Monk, made Duke of Albemarle by a grateful Charles II after the General had organized the King's return to his throne* (Radio Times Hulton Picture Library)

more skilfully than home affairs, though his wars were costly and left his government in serious financial difficulties. Yet this is to leave Scotland and Ireland out of the account, and although it was during the Protectorate that they were first united with England under a single Parliament, they were still foreign countries, and the Cromwellian military occupation did nothing to reconcile either country to permanent union. The Scots with no insuperable religious barrier eventually forgot their animosity, but in Ireland Cromwell's policy of frightfulness has never been forgotten. The massacres of Drogheda and Wexford remain ineradicable stains upon his record.

Clarendon, no favourable critic, sums up Cromwell's influence abroad: 'But his greatness at home was but a shadow of the glory he had abroad. France, Spain, or the Low Countries, where his friendship was current at the value he put upon it. And as they did all sacrifice their honour and their interest to his pleasure, so there is nothing he could have demanded that either of them would have denied him.'

Cromwell the soldier deserves far more respect than Cromwell

the statesman. There are those who rate him among the greatest British generals, but this is going too far. He cannot seriously bear comparison with Marlborough or Wellington; with Montgomery or Slim. Even so his *œuvre* is very respectable. At Marston Moor and Naseby he was not in supreme command, but Preston, Dunbar and Worcester make a trio of victories which few British commanders can rival. The Worcester campaign is evidence of real strategical insight. Dunbar is a masterpiece of tactical skill. In the field of personnel selection also he set precedents that were not to be followed again in the British Army until this century. Men like Harrison, Pride and Hewson, low-born and ill-bred, would not have been commissioned at any time before the First World War. Men like these were for the most part very ill-fitted to administer the eleven districts ruled by the Major-Generals, and made the standing army an object of hatred for centuries after their time. Nevertheless they were shrewd hard-fighting men—'men that know what they fight for, and love what they know' as Cromwell called his 'Ironsides'.

So much for the Statesman and the Soldier. What of the Man? Every Englishman who takes the slightest interest in the great events of the mid-seventeenth century knows full well which side he would have been on at Marston Moor. If one is a Roundhead Cromwell is in Milton's phrase 'our chief of men'. But if you are for the King you may prefer Clarendon's view that 'he had all the wickedness against which damnation is denounced and for which hell-fire is prepared', but even the old Royalist minister recognized that Cromwell 'had some virtues which have caused the memory of some men in all ages to be celebrated', though his conclusion was that Oliver would be 'looked upon by posterity as a brave bad man'. Whatever one thinks of the cause for which he fought, of the execution of the King, Sir Henry Slingsby and others, of the massacres in Ireland and the rule of the Major-Generals, one must recognize his qualities. As Clarendon put it:

> . . . he could never have done half that mischieve without great parts of courage and industry and judgment. And he must have had a wonderful understanding in the natures and humours of men, and as great a dexterity in the applying them, who from a private and obscure birth, (though of a good family), without interest of estate, alliance or friendships, could raise himself to such a height. . . .

54. *Oliver Cromwell's statue standing in front of the Palace of Westminster and the Houses of Parliament* (L.C.C. Photo Library)

OLIVER
CROMWELL
1599
1658

# Summary of Events

1599: 25 April: Born at Huntingdon
1616: 23 April: Matriculates
1617: June: Leaves Sidney Sussex College, Cambridge, on father's death
1620: 22 Aug.: Marries Elizabeth Bourchier
1621: Eldest son, Robert, born
1623: Son, Oliver, born
1624: Daughter, Bridget, born
1625: Charles I becomes king
1626: Son, Richard, born
1628: Son, Henry, born
1629: Daughter, Elizabeth, born
Elected to Parliament as member for Huntingdon
1631: Moves to farm at St Ives, Hunts.
1635: Ship Money case
1636: Opposes King over fen drainage
1637: Daughter, Mary, born
1638: Feb.: Scots sign National Covenant
Daughter, Frances, born
1639: First Bishops War
1640: 5 April: Short Parliament summoned
5 May: Short Parliament dissolved
3 Nov.: Long Parliament begins
30 Dec.: Moves second reading of Triennial Act
1641: 9 Feb.: Violent attack on Bishops
May: Involved in another dispute over fen drainage
Nov.: Irish Rebellion breaks out
22 Nov.: Grand Remonstrance carried
1642: King leaves Westminster for York
Parliament counters with Nineteen Propositions

Aug.: King raises standard at Nottingham
Captain. The Edgehill campaign
1643: 13 May: Colonel. Action at Grantham
29 July: Action at Gainsborough
Governor of the Isle of Ely
Sept.: Solemn League and Covenant signed with Scots
11 Oct.: Lt.-General
Winceby fight
1644: 6 May: Storming of Lincoln
2 July: Battle of Marston Moor
27 Oct.: Second Battle of Newbury
9 Dec.: Speaks in favour of Self-Denying Ordinance, paving way for New Model Army
1645: 24 April: Action near Islip
26 April: Takes Bletchington House
29 April: Repulsed at Faringdon Castle
10 May: Self-Denying Ordinance
14 June: Battle of Naseby
10 July: Battle of Langport
23 July: Surrender of Bridgwater
10 Sept.: Storming of Bristol
8 Oct.: Captures Winchester
14 Oct.: Storming of Basing House
17 Oct.: Captures Langford House
1646: 16 Feb.: Battle of Torrington
Moves household to London
1647: March: Parliament attempts to disband Army
2 June: Cornet Joyce seizes King for Army
June: The Declaration signed
Heads of the Proposals drafted

1647: 10 Aug.: Army enters London
  26 Dec.: Charles I and Scottish Commissioners conclude the Engagement
1648: Second Civil War
  11 July: Captures Pembroke Castle
  17 Aug.: Battle of Preston
1649: 20 Jan.: Trial of Charles I begins
  30 Jan.: Execution of Charles I
  Irish Campaign
  10 Sept.: Storms Drogheda
  Oct.: Storms Wexford
  19 Oct.: Takes Ross
  2 Dec.: Compelled to raise siege of Waterford
1650: Feb.: Takes Cashel and Cahir
  9 May: O'Neill's garrison escapes from Clonmel
  10 May: Surrender of Clonmel
  June: Campaign in Scotland
  3 Sept.: Battle of Dunbar
  Takes Edinburgh

1651: 20 July: Battle of Inverkeithing
  3 Sept.: Battle of Worcester
1652: War between England and the Dutch
1653: 20 April: Expels the Rump of the Long Parliament
  July: Barebones Parliament
  12 Dec.: Parliament resigns power to Lord General
  16 Dec.: Becomes Lord Protector
1654: Alliance with Portugal
  Summer: First Parliament of the Protectorate
1655: 22 Jan.: Parliament dissolved
  March: Penruddock's Rising
  Rule of the Major-Generals
  Decimation Tax
1657: Jan.: Rejects offer of the crown
1658: Jan.: New Upper House elected to Second Parliament
  Jan.: Parliament dissolved
  3 Sept.: Dies

55. *Action off Dover, 1652, during the war with the Dutch* (Radio Times Hulton Picture Library)

# A Select Bibliography

Abbott, W. C. *Writings and Speeches of Oliver Cromwell*, 4 vols., 1937–47

Ashley, Maurice. *The Greatness of Oliver Cromwell*, 1957

Burne, Lt.-Colonel A. H., and Young, Lt.-Colonel P., *The Great Civil War. A Military History*, 1959

Clarendon, Earl of. *The History of the Rebellion and Civil War in England*, Ed. W. D. Macray, Oxford, 1888

Firth, C. H. *Oliver Cromwell*, Heroes of the Nations Series, 1900

Fisher, H. A. L. *A History of Europe*, 1936

Hill, Christopher. *Oliver Cromwell*, Historical Association Pamphlet, 1958

Trevelyan, G. M. *England under the Stuarts*, 1904

Wedgwood, C. V. *The King's Peace*, 1955

―― *The King's War*, 1959

―― *The Trial of Charles I*, 1962

Young, Peter. *Oliver Cromwell and His Times*, 1962